AF674102

The Nature of Things

A Simple Analysis of the Physical World and Things Pertaining to Human Life

The Nature of Things

A Simple Analysis of the Physical World and Things Pertaining to Human Life

Dev Rakhah

PUBLISHING FOR ONE WORLD

NEW AGE INTERNATIONAL (P) LIMITED, PUBLISHERS

(formerly Wiley Eastern Limited)

New Delhi • Bangalore • Chennai • Cochin • Guwahati • Hyderabad
Jalandhar • Kolkata • Lucknow • Mumbai • Ranchi

Visit us at **www.newagepublishers.com**

Copyright © 2007, New Age International (P) Ltd., Publishers
Published by New Age International (P) Ltd., Publishers
First Edition: 2007
Reprint: 2008

All rights reserved.
No part of this book may be reproduced in any form, by photostat, microfilm, xerography, or any other means, or incorporated into any information retrieval system, electronic or mechanical, without the written permission of the copyright owner.

Branches:

- 36, Malikarjuna Temple Street, Opp. ICWA, Basavanagudi, **Bangalore**. ✆ (080) 26677815
- 26, Damodaran Street, T. Nagar, **Chennai**. ✆ (044) 24353401
- Hemsen Complex, Mohd. Shah Road, Paltan Bazar, Near Starline Hotel, **Guwahati**. ✆ (0361) 2543669
- No. 105, 1st Floor, Madhiray Kaveri Tower, 3-2-19, Azam Jahi Road, Nimboliadda, **Hyderabad**. ✆ (040) 24652456
- RDB Chambers (Formerly Lotus Cinema) 106A, Ist Floor, S.N. Banerjee Road, **Kolkata**. ✆ (033) 22275247
- 18, Madan Mohan Malviya Marg, **Lucknow**. ✆ (0522) 2209578
- 142C, Victor House, Ground Floor, N.M. Joshi Marg, Lower Parel, **Mumbai**. ✆ (022) 24927869
- 22, Golden House, Daryaganj, **New Delhi**. ✆ (011) 23262370, 23262368

ISBN (10) : 81-224-2141-5
ISBN (13) : 978-81-224-2141-5

Rs. 195.00/ US $ 8.00/ U.K. £ 3.99

C-08-10-3165

Printed in India at Ramprintograph, Delhi.
Typeset at in-house

PUBLISHING FOR ONE WORLD
NEW AGE INTERNATIONAL (P) LIMITED, PUBLISHERS
4835/24, Ansari Road, Daryaganj, New Delhi-110002
Visit us at **www.newagepublishers.com**

FOREWORD

The author has written very rightly that this book will be very useful to those readers, especially during the early age of their life. But I am happy to say that even at the age of 67 at present, I have benefited enormously after reading the draft of this book. This book is a very good guide. It gives some very important lessons of life to everybody – irrespective of age and background.

The book, *"The Nature of Things"* is a very useful, informative, readable, and guiding and inspiring for readers of all ages. It is directly related to human life, its problems, tensions, decisions and the temperaments in our modern society. The writer has studied very seriously in depth the nature of human beings and the society in which we live as well as the influence of past traditions and beliefs on us. He has found that we generally live in this world by others' directions and decisions, and as a result we cannot develop our own consciousness – what is right and what is wrong. But it is essential to develop our own consciousness and the power to take appropriate decisions, independently.

The present science, psychology and other knowledge of the modern world has changed the mindset of the human being, and we should adopt this knowledge for the true happiness in our life. The writer wants the readers to see things in the right directions and from the right perspectives, so that the right decisions can be taken, eventually. This book gives the reader the basic understanding of life; it is geared towards the betterment of mankind. It explains so clearly: how certain things arise, develop and affect our life.

I hope this book will kindle some awareness among the readers and will also give them an insight of the real nature of things. I am sure the readers will feel that they are living a better life after reading it.

I congratulate Shri Dev Rakhah for writing this marvelous book – a must read – for readers of all age groups. Undoubtedly, they will be inspired by its scientific, philosophical and psychological analysis of life to be an open-minded and modern human being.

Dr. Kamal Kishore Goyanka
Ashok Vihar
New Delhi

Preface

Man is always in the quest for something – for better living, more happiness, etc. – but in unawareness he ends up in undesirable situations. Most of the time, we are ourselves responsible for our sufferings. We ignore the fundamental principles and the natural laws, and yet, we expect everything to be okay. That is simply not possible; the universe does not revolve around our sweet wishes; there are certain principles and laws in existence, and we are all subjected to them; we are all governed by them.

The dust of ages is blurring our vision. To believe dogmatically anything, is wrong and dangerous. In this so-called modern age, however, we are still blinded by beliefs and rituals; we are still indulging in absurdities and vulgar superstitions, which have no meaning in actuality. What the world needs, is not dogma but an attitude of objective inquiry.

We depend too much on thoughts of others; we take for granted ideas from peers and society; we are yielding to dubious practices without bothering to ask any question. Consequently, humans are merely existing as non-entities; they cannot think in total independence; they have adopted a herd mentality, and in despair, are falling prey in increasing numbers to unscrupulous predators.

Sometimes, borrowed thoughts can be useful but they can be harmful too, if accepted without scrutiny and implemented blindly. One's intelligence gets suppressed under borrowed ideas, and by over dependence on them.

Ready-made answers and second-hand solutions are of little help to problems arising from inside. One has to dig out for solutions within oneself; truth has to come from within oneself. Truth cannot be learned, it has to be uncovered and experienced. By the way, it is not by meaningless accumulation of facts that one becomes a man of wisdom – no; truth cannot be known by such superficial means.

In blindness, we have a tendency to hold on to beliefs; we pay attention only to things and practices that suit our prejudices. It is like shunning the fountain of life, to cling to the material body. Damnation is mistaken for salvation!

People are protecting systems that are intrinsically anti-progressive and non-evolutionary; they are still glorifying retrograde customs and traditions with unabated enthusiasm. Usually people resist change; they prefer status quo. But rigid attitudes and behaviour are not conducive to growth and evolution. Fixed paradigms or mindsets are of very little use, if we want to move forward.

So if we are not careful, we move away from truth, instead of coming near it. But once we get insight and eyesight, we become free from the veil of ignorance; the whole mystery shrouding existence will no longer be a total mystery.

Knowledge is of two types: transcendental and non-transcendental. Transcendental knowledge operates in the purely spiritual world, and therefore derives its inspiration from the Cosmic centre. This type of knowledge inspires people to move in the purely spiritual world; it also inspires them with countless elevating spiritual ideas; it leads to self-realization.

In our physical world, we cannot think of life without science. Nevertheless, science has its own limitations with its mechanistic and empirical approach. It can describe processes; it does not explain the 'why' of processes; it is outside its purview. Moreover, there is no scientific answer to every question. To fully understand existence, we have to go beyond the limits of science.

In this book, the main concern is non-transcendental knowledge – knowledge pertaining to our material world and the nature of things therein. Incidentally, a lot of what the reader will come across is not new information. However, there are so many things, hitherto forgotten or ignored probably. With better knowledge and understanding of existence, we can relate more effectively with whatever thing we have to put up with in this world.

The value of an idea is directly proportional to its potential power. Nothing is more powerful than an idea, the time of which has come. Certain ideas, if properly understood and scientifically applied can transform the world; they are the ruling stars in the firmament that will guide humanity towards its development and realization. The idea that has impacted the scientific world beyond imagination is most probably, the one from Einstein's theory of relativity; it has almost transformed our very concept of the physical world.

An attempt is made to highlight some ideas which are very pertinent to our lives, and are relevant at all times.

My aim is to caution all those travellers in this earthly sojourn, so that they do not get entrapped by the various snares and pitfalls, they will inevitably come across. Of course, it serves no purpose to read a book on travel at the end of a journey; for any benefit one has to read it in the beginning. Once forewarned, and subsequently with a heightened sense of awareness, one is then expected to surmount any obstacle on the way.

So it is hoped that the pieces of advice and the time-tested statements highlighted in this book, will be of considerable help to all those well-intentioned people who would like to improve their living conditions and those of others in this world.

Dev Rakhah

d.rakhah@intnet.mu

www.consciousway.org

Acknowledgments and Dedication

I am grateful to all writers and teachers who have inspired me throughout my life.

I am very particularly grateful to Dr. K. K. Goyanka for his exhortation to write this book, and for his valuable Foreword.

I am thankful to Mr. Bhoomithtre Boolell and Mrs. Doolaree Nuckcheddy for their valuable comments.

My deepest respect to late Dr. Philip George Owston who was my chemistry tutor in U.K. and late Robert Atwell of South Africa, who gave me some priceless tips on healthy living.

My dedication and indebtedness to my parents: late father Nunkiswur Rakhah and late mother Jassodah Gungadin for the upbringing care and protection as well as the early lessons of life.

CONTENTS

INTRODUCTION

The entire world and everything in it has a particular form. In fact, every finite thing has a form; it is also conditioned by space and time. Being perishable in nature, it is bound to undergo change, according to the laws governing it. The world itself is in a state of flux. In existence, creation, sustenance, evolution and destruction are a normal state of affairs.

> ***"Weep not that the world changes – did it keep a stable, changeless state, it were cause indeed to weep."***
>
> ***William Cullen Bryant***

It is foolish to expect security in a world subject to constant change since its creation; indeed, if there is anything that is certain in an unstable and transitory world, it is: uncertainty. Moreover, there has never been any status quo, in so far as evolution is concerned; nothing is at a standstill. As incredible as it may seem, no two moments are identical. Indeed, if there were no perpetual change, there would be no life on earth.

> ***"The world's a scene of changes, and to be Constant, in Nature were inconstancy."***
>
> ***Abraham Cowley***

Life is incomprehensibly and terrifyingly complex in a world which is apparently becoming more and more chaotic. Life is also in a perpetual state of motion; it is so, because of endless desires. The will of man is made up of desires. There is no such thing as absolute tranquillity of the mind. From birth to death, the mind is in a continuous state of motion.

CHANGEABLE AND NON-CHANGEABLE THINGS

1

In this physical world, there are changeable things and non-changeable things too. It is for us to know the difference; we should distinguish the possible from the impossible. It is better to forget things that are impossible to change.

We have to come to terms with inevitable changes; we must build up nerves of steel in powerful and elastic muscles, in order to be able to endure anything, whenever it is unavoidable.

The whole world seems to be in a perpetual state of turmoil since its creation; it is ever changing; nothing is static. There is a multitude of natural phenomena happening all the time: earthquakes, tsunamis, volcanoes, hurricanes, cyclones, tornadoes, thunder-storms, floods, landslides, avalanches, droughts, forest fires, etc. Natural calamities are almost omnipresent. It is difficult to conceive a single region, unaffected by anyone of the phenomena mentioned; only few places in this globe manifest relative tranquillity. There are so many imponderables that it is almost impossible to make predictions, and yet nothing can happen just by chance.

If some of the natural phenomena look supernatural or unnatural, it is due to our limited knowledge. There is no such thing as supernatural, per se; it is because of our insufficiency of understanding that we are perplexed by them.

In an ever-changing world, man should abstain from interfering in the plan of nature; he should not block the processes of nature; he should not create unnecessary problems. Instead, he should learn how to ride over nature's waves with dexterity; fighting against them is futile. The direction of the wind cannot be changed, but we can adjust our sails.

Most of the ills of society were not predetermined; they are the results of man's immature and thoughtless living. But, what are the causes of suffering? The following quote will help us considerably:

> ***"The chessboard is the world; the pieces are the phenomena of the Universe; the rules of the game are what we call the laws of Nature. The player on the other side is hidden from us. We know that his play is always fair and patient. But also we know, to our cost that he never overlooks a mistake, or makes the smallest allowance for ignorance."***
>
> ***Thomas Henry Huxley***

Of course, no one wishes to be a victim of any calamity, and most people prefer stability in their lives. So, it is absolutely imperative for us to understand the various laws governing the physical, chemical and biological world, if we want to survive with serenity. The fundamental laws and principles do not change; we have to adapt ourselves to them. Therefore, it behoves us to observe and study them, if we do not wish to be adversely affected.

THE UNIVERSAL LAWS AND PRINCIPLES

2

All things in existence – the material universe and the various life forms in it are governed by the Universal Laws and Principles. Once the laws and principles are known and understood, one can live in harmony; every detail of life will make sense; all the events therein can be related to one another.

There are several laws and principles; they are all inter-connected; without them there could be no harmony in existence. The Universal Principles pertain to the creation of life and its sustenance, whereas the Universal Laws govern everything.

THE PRINCIPLE OF CREATION

Creation is a process; it comprises things and events based on a certain principle. All things and phenomena are in a state of vibration; it is an unending process. In any vibratory process, polarities are involved. Polarities can be like as well as unlike in nature; without polarities there is no creation. Polarized particles interact in different ways. Particles of similar polarity repel one another, whereas particles of opposite polarities attract one another.

Once we know the degree and nature of polarity – whether positive or negative – of reacting particles, we can predict the outcome of the product(s). The greater the difference in polarity of the reacting particles, the more violent reactions we can expect.

For example, sodium metal which is very electropositive, reacts explosively with highly electronegative chlorine gas to form sodium chloride – a neutral substance. Sodium chloride is the main component of common salt used in the kitchen.

Incidentally, the same principle is manifest everywhere in existence. Indeed, it may be considered as the blueprint for creation. The principle which applies to inanimate things is also applicable to animals and plants.

Most flowers have both male and female parts, known as the androecium and the gynoecium, respectively. The male cells are present in pollen grains, whereas the female cells are found in the ovules enclosed in a structure known as the ovary. Through the process of pollination – done by insects and wind usually – the pollen grains from the androecium are transferred to the gynoecium for fusion with the female cells in the ovules. As a result of the fusion, that is, fertilization we get seeds; the seeds are enclosed in the ovary which later becomes a fruit.

The same principle is to be found in the case of animals. In most animals the male and female parts are in separate bodies. However, in hermaphrodites such as snails and earthworms, both the male and female parts are present in the same body. Whether the male and female parts are present in different bodies or not, the principle of polarities does not change. In human species also, we have opposite polarities; an offspring is the result of interaction of cells with opposite polarities. So polarity is pivotal in creation.

In Tao philosophy, the opposite polarities are known as yin and yang – yin as feminine and yang as masculine. Other examples of opposites representing yin and yang are: black and white, night and day, etc.

The Universal Law of Causation

The law of causation is probably the most pervasive of all. It is universal; all cosmic bodies, animals and plants conform exclusively to it. This law operates with a disconcerting precision, both in the physical and mental planes.

There is a definite connection between what is happening now and the events to come. For every cause there is an effect. And for every action there is a reaction; the reaction will be of equal force and of similar nature.

> *"Everything in nature is a cause from which there flows an effect."*
>
> **Baruch Spinoza**

In fact, no event occurs without a cause somewhere hidden at the back of it, that is, no phenomenon can escape the law of causation. Every happening has its own cause.

We cannot afford to ignore the fundamental law governing the universe, if we wish to exercise control in our lives.

It is difficult to separate a cause from its effect. For example, when a seed sprouts into a plant, that is, it is the cause for the plant, which can be then regarded as an effect. Likewise, the plant which produces the seeds, becomes the cause for the seeds. There is no uniformity as far as seed growth is concerned; some seeds germinate within a few hours whereas some others of a different variety take several weeks. We cannot expect a lily bulb to grow at the same pace as an acorn of an oak tree! Be that as it may, the cause is inherent in the effect; it is found in the effect, and vice-versa. And as a result, we get a chain of cause and effect.

The law of causation includes the law of action and reaction, the law of compensation and the law of retribution. All these laws operate together; they are all interconnected.

Unfortunately a lot of people do not take heed of the universal laws mentioned; to many others, the whole cosmos is manifesting myriads of mind-boggling things by pure chance – that is a very unscientific approach. True, there are many things which look accidental at a cursory glance. Nevertheless, nothing is accidental per se; it looks accidental if we do not know the cause. But any open-minded person, who just watches the movements of waves at the seaside, will know that, the wind is behind the waves. And behind the wind, which consists of air, there is something else, and so on. Every effect has a cause behind it.

Similarly, no one is born alcoholic or a drug addict. It is only through bad influence that one becomes a victim. One may not become a drug addict overnight, but negative acquaintances can only turn out to be liabilities.

Sometimes, we are unable to connect an effect from its exact cause; the effect can be perceptible, but with no apparent cause and vice-versa. Therefore, we are baffled by the apparent incoherence; things seem to be so irrational, uncoordinated, and even chaotic. Well, that does not mean there is no connection; we have to blame our ignorance – not the omnipresent universal laws.

The law of causation does not seem to be as palpable as some other laws such as the laws of gravitation, the laws of cycles, etc. The law of gravitation, for example, is now quite evident to us following Isaac Newton's observation of the falling apple. Of course, the law existed well before Newton discovered it; people were simply unaware of it. Now, it is common knowledge that, if we throw a stone towards the sky, it comes back due to the force of gravity. In the same manner, the law of causation is also a reality, although its operational mechanism is not so palpable, in some cases. Whether we pay attention or not, we cannot escape from the effect of a cause, as long as we are connected to this world. Whether we act consciously or unconsciously, the result cannot be averted; it makes no difference. For example, a child who put his hands into fire will get burned; there can be only one outcome. He will definitely learn from the effects the hard way, and hopefully, he will avoid making mistakes in future.

So, every thought or action has its consequences – whether good or bad – but the human idea of the respective reward or punishment does not have to correspond to the way things happen in the Cosmos. In Existence, things do not necessarily happen according to human principles of logic; things do not happen according to human fancies and sweet wishes; our demands do not get gratified instantaneously. Indeed, most of the time, the subtle and inscrutable ways of existence are beyond the ken of ordinary minds; it is not even surprising to come across seemingly paradoxical situations.

The moral law of cause and effect wherein an individual is given precisely what he earns is known as **Karma** – a Sanskrit word. He gets what he deserves and deserves what he gets. For instance, we do not expect a bad action to give good results, and conversely, a good action cannot give evil results. Whatever we sow, we reap accordingly. The seed that we sow eventually grows into a tree –initially involuted and contained in the former. So, the effect may be considered as something – even before its manifestation – contained in the cause. Indeed, the relation between evolution and involution is an inseparable one. The fact that we cannot get something out of nothing, established as a scientific fact, we can therefore infer that involution precedes evolution.

It should be borne in mind that any form of compensation or retribution does not have to be instantaneous – there is a time lag. And the time lag is determined by the resultant of the interplay of all other causes and effects. By the way each individual is unique; he is born with his own reserve of Karma. Therefore, it is almost impossible to forecast with precision the time of maturity of any particular cause, and trying to find some logic in terms of external happenings only, is unrealistic. Outward happenings of life usually do not manifest coherence to the observer.

The law of Karma explains life based on the principle of reincarnation or transmigration of the soul. It means that our present situation, that is, physical, financial, health, parents, friends, etc. is a function of the resultant of the overall number of cumulative actions we have performed in the past lives, prior to this present incarnation. Thus, we are the product of the interplay of cumulative causes and effects. And the future is determined by what we already are and what we desire in the present. Any wrongly conceived action will give rise to an undesirable effect; the effect may well be a disastrous one.

So it is better to abstain from committing blunders because sooner or later we are bound to reap the respective effects. The effect of mistakes is inevitable. The question of getting away scot-free or wheeling back does not arise. Anyway, it is beyond the scope of this booklet to delve into Karma and all the metaphysical aspects.

Thus, it is important to understand the nature of things of this world – the various laws governing the world and the various phenomena therein. Only then we will be properly equipped to manage our problems; only then we will reach our destinations in spite of the various pitfalls on the way. Some people may not be religious, but the laws of nature cannot be brushed aside without detrimental consequences. At every step, we must exercise our faculty of discrimination. So, always minding the universal laws and principles will spare us a lot of unnecessary troubles.

3

Goals and Means

It is good to set goals, but we must pay attention to the means too. One should pay attention to the means, that is, the causes; only then one can expect reaching the end with confidence and serenity. The end or the effect does not come all right by itself, and if the cause is improper, we cannot expect the effect to be proper. So if we take sufficient heed of the cause, we do not have to worry about the effect. In other words, everything boils down to the way, we manage the initial cause.

The realization of any objective or goal may be regarded as the effect. The means are the causes, and when they are just, the results also are bound to be just.

> ***"Cause and effect, means and ends, seed and fruit cannot be severed."***
>
> ***Ralph Waldo Emerson***

One may have recourse to foul means to arrive at the end, but the satisfaction one gets with proper means is beyond comparison. It is good to hold important positions but not by deceit; the obstacles met and the manner they are overcome, are very important. It is a lot more honourable to achieve even a little, but by fair means, than achieving a lot, by unfair and reprehensible means. To attain anything commendable, one has to strive and struggle with might. Moreover, one must entertain positive thoughts. Those having recourse to foul means would do well to do some inward-looking, that is, some introspection before boasting of any 'achievement'.

If we sow and nurture a seed by providing the best conditions, we can undoubtedly end up with a healthy plant. The huge banyan tree is obtained from a tiny seed; the seed carries the blueprint of the entire tree; it germinates slowly to give a huge tree. Of course, it is possible only if we have all the right conditions. We cannot just throw it on a dry rock and expect to get a fully developed tree. We need to find a suitable place: there must be sufficient water and nutrients in the soil; there has to be enough sunshine and air as well. So when the means are taken care of, the end is not too far away.

A coconut tree growing in the shade is not going to bear fruits. But when the tree is taken care of, flowers will bloom at the right time; there is no need to focus on the flowering process; it will appear on its own. When the means are right, the fruits of harvest will also be sweet.

By the way, it is important for an effect to be causally related. Evidently, means can only produce effects; of course, if the means themselves have the intrinsic potential to do so. If it were not so, we could obtain sesame oil from sand; or we could obtain butter by churning water!

Usually, an effect is not totally different from its respective means. In fact, it is essentially the same; it is engrained in the means. For example, wooden furniture has more or less, the same physical and chemical properties as the plain wood, from which it is made; it is just a sort of rearrangement of matter.

Everything is good for something. All the terrestrial things around us may be regarded as means. But if they are not properly understood, the same means could become hindrances; a helper can also become a nuisance.

4 Reaching the Goal with Right Steps

It is a bit natural to achieve results, without bothering too much with regard to input. We are tempted to circumvent normal procedures to achieve our objectives as quickly as possible. However, there are certain things that must be respected, if we want to get good results. We should not expect to get satisfactory results by perfunctory methods. For example, pure gold can be obtained from its ore, only by the right chemical and physical processes.

No fine work can be done without concentration and diligence – nothing worthwhile is achieved. Haste makes waste, and waste in turn creates uneasiness and guilt. It takes less time to do something properly than messing it up in haste, and then trying to do it over again. Therefore, it is better not to be in unnecessary haste; it is better not to precipitate matters. As goes the saying: slow and steady wins the race.

We must give time to time. Any construction project, however huge, has a starting point somewhere. Rome was not built in a day. Stone by stone a wall is erected. Many a little makes a mickle, that is, small amounts accumulate to make a large amount. With small rivulets we end up with a raging river.

So patience and endurance are a must, when one is set to achieve something worthwhile. It is also from little acorn that we get an oak tree, and also little strokes fell great oaks. Perhaps it is important to ponder on one of the famous sayings of Lao Tzu:

> ***"A journey of a thousand miles must begin with a single step."***

We have to start somewhere. Of course, if the direction is wrong, we will drift further away from the goal. A slight inaccuracy at the outset, can lead to miles away from the destination.

If we want to extract the hidden oil from a seed, we have to go through the right processes; if we want to see the hidden fire from flint stone, vigorous rubbing is required; if we want to eat food, cooking has to be done.

Similarly, if we are to unfold the mystery of existence and acquire knowledge, we must remove the veils of ignorance from our life. It is not by drinking ink that one becomes a knowledgeable person. Knowledge will come only, if we try hard to get it, through learning; only then we can drive away ignorance; a rusted iron-like mind is turned into gold only by the right method.

Furthermore, distillation and crystallization of great thoughts take place at their own pace; they also happen in conducive environments; the state of the mind has to be positive and undisturbed. So for formation of things, we must get the right conditions – the right parameters.

We come near our goal by taking the right steps only. Hasty climbers have spectacular falls. The ascension of any ladder is a stepwise process. The climb of the highest mountain starts from its base. One should not be on the look out for short cuts all the time or else one might run the risk of getting cut-shorted for good.

Are We the Masters of Our Destiny?

5

Some people feel that everything has already been decided – even our future; we have no control in anything whatsoever; we are just puppets because there are so many things totally beyond our control. For example, we say that we do not choose to be born; we do not choose our birth place; we do not choose our parents and relatives; we have no choice over the colour of our skin; we have no choice over our intelligence. Moreover, there are so many things which have been happening in our lives without our ever having any choice; we have no say, no will over them; we have no will over our existence. We think that things do not necessarily happen the way we hope them to happen, and that we are helpless in the jaws of fate. So, to admit that we are the absolute masters of our destiny, seems to be quite illogical.

All outward happenings and manifestations, however, do not always have their reasons outside. We are wonder-struck only if we cannot relate the surface happenings to the inner needs – the needs of the inner being. In fact, nothing happens by mere chance. Man is a product of the cumulative effect of all his thoughts, desires and actions.

Therefore, one's present destiny is the net result of one's all past activities; it depends entirely on the quality of the past activities, according to the law of Karma.

We know that we can exercise our limited free-will to acquire many things in life namely: wealth, name, fame and status. We can mould our lives in the way we like; we can change our lifestyle; we can achieve many things. But, by exercising a certain amount of free-will in certain specific areas only, we cannot accomplish everything in life. Obviously, all the areas we deliberately neglect will remain atrophied; nothing will just come out of the blue; there can be no output without any input.

So those who think they have no control on their lives, probably overlook some undeniable facts. How to explain the inequalities since birth, for instance? True, we may be equal before the law, but we are far from equal in many respects. For instance, we must admit that we do not have the same physical and mental potential of development. Some people are born with a manifesting huge potential, right at the very outset; their destinations can be almost extrapolated.

The law of life enables us to understand the process of evolution. Once it is grasped, we can explain the apparent diversity and inequality seen everywhere. There must be some reason; the differences among human beings are the effects of causes which lie imbedded and ingrained in the character of each individual.

Thus, the law of karma becomes very plausible in explaining our destiny.

So, if one intensely desires something and makes the necessary efforts to acquire it, eventually one is not denied it. In fact, desires are like the seeds of new births and the nature of those desires shapes our future. If the spirit is earnest and full of yearning, nothing can prevent us from getting what we deserve. At the end of the struggle, there has to be some sort of crystallization. In case of any failure, there must have been some sort of omission somewhere. One has to correct one's mistakes and try and try again.

In Existence, things happen according to certain rules – dreams do not materialize instantaneously like instant coffee. But at the end of the day, everything should fall into its place; it is a question of genuine deserving and time.

Destiny is the net result of all our previous and present efforts. If the previous and present efforts are contrary in nature, then the stronger one will determine the destiny. Thus, we make and unmake our destiny by our thoughts and actions; we shape our future by our current thinking and actions. Nothing happens at random; nothing is adventitious. Existence always responds in right measure to our deserving wishes.

In a certain way as someone had said: "Life is a do-it-yourself project." Our attitudes and the choices we make today, build the 'house' that we live in tomorrow. So, if we have to build anything, it is better to build wisely. Of course, it is important to proportion our ambitions according to our capacities, at any given point in time.

Don't Blame your Stars

It is very common to see people believing in good luck or bad luck. For the enlightened one, that is, the one who understands the law of cause and effect and the nature of worldly phenomena, there is no such thing as luck.

> ***"Shallow men believe in luck. Strong men believe in cause and effect."***
>
> ***Ralph Waldo Emerson***

We are largely responsible for our state of being; it is of no use attributing any success or failure to the stars and planets. Every man is the architect of his own fortune; he carries his destiny in his own hands.

If we become strong enough, we can convert unfavourable circumstances into favourable ones. We should not concede defeat because of preconceived and irrevocable destiny. The will of the inner being determines everything; fate can be changed by an unflinching iron will. Unlike ordinary animals, man has the privilege to mould his own destiny.

We can say that: **what** we come across in life is destiny; but how we come across is free will. Most of the time, we have the free will, that is, the prerogative to trace our own destinations. Thus, it is a question of choice the manner we exercise that free will of ours. Our thoughts, words and deeds are directly linked to our future. So whatever we do now, will certainly have an incidence on our destiny. We cannot escape from that reality.

With time, we will be confronted with the fruits of our actions: there is no question of running away. Existence is neutral; it cannot be tricked or cheated; it cannot be fiddled or bribed. As stated before, the effect is always commensurate with the cause. The quality of the fruits depends on the type of seeds we have sown, that is, the quality of our actions. We cannot contemplate to harvest contrary to the seeds we have sown. Thus, to reap a rich harvest, one has to make the necessary preparation for it. The law of cause and effect is relentless; it is ineluctable; it can neither be abrogated nor contorted.

Our destiny is not governed by some supernatural power. Neither happiness nor misery is enforced arbitrarily upon us. We can only reap the inevitable results of our thoughts and deeds. No supernatural power can prevent us from getting what we have earned. So, it is ultimately the decisions we make that will determine where we end up in life.

Therefore, it is man's own effort which is the determining factor. Man can achieve virtually anything in this world, provided he makes the right effort – in terms of thoughts, words and deeds.

6

We Cannot Reverse the Course of Events

Every beginning has an end. Every step will inexorably lead to its end. The river of life follows its own course. Just as the earth does not change its direction of rotation around the sun, the currents of life also maintain their flow in a determined direction.

On certain matters we can hardly intervene; we can hardly have any impact at all. Therefore, it is futile to struggle against the nature of things. We can only witness things unfolding according to nature; we have to come to terms with them. For instance, water does not flow against gravity; a fallen fruit does not get reattached to a tree; a mature and stiff bamboo cane cannot be reversed into a tender shoot; we cannot recall a fired bullet once we pull the trigger of a gun.

Up to a certain point, we may have some sort of control, but we should not grossly interfere in the processes of nature; we do not have to struggle against a current which can potentially tear us apart. For example, it is absolutely foolish to challenge an avalanche sweeping everything on its way. We do not also expose ourselves to lightning during a thunderstorm and run the risk of getting electrocuted; if we can harness the energy therein, so much the better; otherwise it is better to keep away.

Once a destructive phenomenon is energized and is full of momentum, it is better to remain aloof. If we cannot effectively control a natural phenomenon, we must adjust to it. We must keep our distance and learn to let things follow their own courses; we must let things happen and allow the time and space to get them resolved. A storm, no matter how raging, has to subside after some time; the energy of a thunderbolt has to dissipate somehow. That is the way of nature: to diffuse when there is too much tension, to move from higher energy to lower energy, to move from a high concentration medium to a low concentration medium, to occupy whatever is empty.

Growth and Decay Cannot be Reversed

Changes in life are to be accepted as calmly as the changes in season. Nature bursts forth into blossom after a long morbid winter.

It is the destiny of man to be born, to die and to decay. Birth is followed by youth; youth is followed by old age; old age is followed by death and decay. So while living, there is also a slow dying.

Incidentally, without growth and decay, there is no perpetuation of life. Species are best preserved, when seeds are allowed to grow. It sounds paradoxical, and yet that is how things are. It is only after growth and flowering that, seeds can be obtained in large numbers. Thus, a seed is best preserved by allowing it to die into a fertile soil; only after death and decay that it will be reborn into a new plant, and so on.

Even celestial bodies do have a beginning and an end; creation, sustenance and destruction of planets are natural phenomena of the universe. Our whole solar system will come to its dissolution, some time in the future.

There is no such thing like, physical immortality. Also, the end of one thing leads to the beginning of another. Such is the course of life – the nature of things. According to Vedanta, life is a form of consciousness; it originates from something to end up into something else. But life does not end with the disintegration of the physical body; it dissolves into existence. The physical body dissolves into its basic constituents, but the mental being does not change; its essence is not lost; it passes into other forms in existence – it cannot vanish into nothingness. And from existence, life bubbles up again and so on.

Verily, death is only a process which enables life to perpetuate; death is implicit in life; birth is impossible without death. Indeed, birth may be regarded as the beginning of death. Even though birth and death are opposites, they are inseparable. It is only an apparent separateness; it only looks that way. Birth and death may be compared to day and night – dependent upon each other; day cannot exist without night, and vice-versa.

So, birth and death are expressions of the same thing, looked from different viewpoints; they are the two ends of the same thing – two manifestations of the same reality; they are like the rising and falling of the same wave, in the same ocean; they are the evaporating water and the condensing water vapour of the same substance. There is no beginning and no ending; the beginning is in the end and vice-versa.

There is no such thing like physical immortality. Also, the end of one thing is also the beginning of another. This is the course of life — the nature of things. According to Vedanta, life is a journey to [illegible] ... [illegible]

[illegible]

The Intrinsic Nature of the Foundation is the Same

7

The intrinsic nature of the foundation is the same since time immemorial. Certain things are quite natural as they are. In case we are stupefied upon discovering their nature, indeed, that can only highlight our ignorance. There is nothing new since time immemorial.

For example, elements and compounds have their properties – whatever they are – since creation. We are the ones who were in ignorance, and now we are grappling to take cognizance of them. If until recently, the formula of water was unknown, it does not mean anything to nature. But, of course to us, it means a lot. Now we know: two atoms of hydrogen and one atom of oxygen combine together to form one molecule of water(H_2O) .

In the not so distant past, we had a totally different concept of matter. Now with the advent of Quantum Mechanics in modern Physics, there is no such thing as matter in the form we were accustomed to. Albert Einstein, Max Planck, Louis de Broglie, Niels Bohr, Werner Heisenberg, Erwin Shrodinger and other scientists unraveled the nature of matter by their most fascinating and conclusive experiments. Hence, our concept of the physical world is lot more closer to reality.

What appears to be solid, in reality consists of minute particles known as atoms. These atoms are made up of smaller sub-particles known as: protons, neutrons and electrons. When we go deeper, there are even other smaller sub-particles! The protons and neutrons are concentrated inside the nucleus of an atom, whereas the fast moving electrons are found in the periphery, in the outermost part of the atom. The speed of the electrons is staggering – about 1000 kms per sec! The electrons zip so fast within such a small space that a sort of solidity appears to be there. In reality, what we have is a lot of space between the nucleus of an atom and the surrounding electrons.

Well, just to get an idea of the amount of empty space inside an atom, we can consider the hydrogen atom which is the lightest and simplest, as an example.

If a hydrogen atom is magnified until its nucleus becomes the size of a ping-pong ball, then its electron will look like a very tiny dust particle spinning and orbiting about 300 metres away. In fact, the actual radius of the electron orbit, i.e. the distance between the nucleus of a hydrogen atom and its electron is an infinitesimal fraction of a centimetre; it is about 0.0000000053 centimetre!

By moving deeper into matter through objective analytical methods, the physicist reaches a point of uncertainty. The electron behaves as a particle as well as a wave.

Atoms of other elements also display similar features because they are made up of the same constituents – the same sub-particles. If elements differ in their properties, it is due to the different number and arrangement of the sub-particles. Each atom vibrates at a particular frequency;

similar feature is to be found in any group of atoms or molecules. Matter may be regarded as the manifestation of energy in a certain form. The form of matter depends on the motion and vibration of the atoms producing it. Stunningly, each atom resembles a planetary system, in miniature, and no two atoms occupy the same position in space. The macrocosm is reflected in the microcosm and vice-versa.

The nutrients sustaining human life are the same since the advent of humans in this planet. We still require carbohydrates, fats, proteins, vitamins, minerals and water for our subsistence; we cannot do away with the fundamental building blocks of life. In spite of all scientific and scintillating technological developments, we are still dependent on the same nutrients. So, being fully aware of that undeniable fact, we cannot afford to poison the elements and compounds, that is, the nutrients indispensable for our survival.

Is Man A Mechanical Entity?

It seems that a lot of people are still in doubt, as regards the foundation of man. Some consider man as a sentient being in the highest scale of evolution so far; he is defined as, just a mass of organized chemicals – nothing more, nothing less. Such a simplistic approach, which discards the spiritual aspect, has a lot of shortcomings, however.

Be that as it may, whatever the conviction, it is totally absurd to regard man as a mechanical machine. He is not just a lump of flesh and bones. The structure may well be chemical in nature, but life itself cannot be manifested by chemicals only; there has to be an indispensable spiritual dimension. It cannot have a material foundation. Although the structure is of material nature, the foundation is not of material nature – it is spiritual.

So, man is not a mechanical entity. He is not a mechanical structure in a mechanical foundation. The different parts and organs of his body are not merely objects; they do not exist in separateness. What we have, is a sentient being, with interlinking of the so-called parts constituting the whole. For example, the brain is linked to the other parts of the body; it does not function as a completely separate organ.

Man has a spiritual foundation with a material structure; his intrinsic nature has not changed.

Right Assessment is Imperative Before Responding

8

"Life is short, the art is long, timing is exact, experience treacherous, judgement difficult."

Hippocrates

Incidentally, by denying the inherent problems pertaining to the world, one cannot wish away with them. But it is also foolish to try to solve a problem, when the cause itself is not fully known, otherwise our so-called solution could become another problem. First and foremost, we need to address to our own ignorance and other inadequacies. Then with proper understanding and knowledge, we can expect to solve the problem. Only by adopting the right attitude and performing our duty in right-awareness that we will manage to reach somewhere.

Very often we react too impulsively. We do not give ourselves a moment of reflection; we do things in inadvertence or by haste, and the more so, wrongly. So we are responsible ourselves for our blunders. But with right assessment, we can act much more reasonably.

For example, one cannot get drowned by sinking in water unless one really works hard at it. Why? Because the nature of water is not to pull things downward; on the contrary, it is to push things upward. The pushing force is known as the upthrust. The denser the water, the greater is its force of upthrust. Thus, water with a high degree of salinity, such as water in the Dead Sea, which is quite dense, exerts a much greater upthrust than the water in the Atlantic Ocean.

Logically therefore, it would be much harder for a person to sink in the Dead Sea than to keep afloat. It is only by yielding to panic and needless agitations that he can expect to be drowned. So one should not struggle thoughtlessly in water; to remain afloat one needs to be relaxed; instead of confronting, one must learn to let things go when and as required.

Similarly, one must respond tactfully when one comes across a ferocious dog. By trying to challenge it, one will worsen matters. The more provocative one becomes the greater the chance of being attacked. The best thing is to remain calm as much as possible; then the probability of avoiding contact with the dog will be much greater.

Sometimes, despite all our efforts, we are still unable to grasp with confidence the nature of a particular matter. Consequently, we do not know how to respond appropriately. Well, in such a situation, we must go for the most sensible and realistic option.

> ***"It is a truth very certain that, when it is not in our power to determine what is true, we ought to follow what is most probable."***
>
> ***Rene Descartes***

Nothing is essentially bad; everything has its importance; there are things which are probably not in their proper places. A stone, suitable to form part of a wall must not be an obstacle on the way. Once each and every thing falls on its true place, there will be a lot of harmony in the world.

If a small pin can do the job of removing a foreign particle from the skin, there in no need to look for a knife. We do not use a sledgehammer to crack chestnuts. Likewise, there is no need to kill butterflies with bullets, neither do we need a tank to kill ants; the force applied should be in proportion of the job to be done. There is no need to hit the head of a needle with a hammer if a spoon can be more effective.

If you are in a forest and a thorn entered your body, there is no need to look for a big knife or needle to remove it; you just take another thorn and remove the first one with it. There is more than one way to kill a cat, anyway. But one has to be conscious of what one is doing: one does not scratch one's shoes when the foot itches!

When we run a high temperature due to fever, we don't try to get rid of the fever by simply bringing down the temperature. Nevertheless, in total confusion, we attempt to reduce the fever by bringing down the temperature – artificially! Instead of attacking the disease at the roots, we have the impulsive tendency to fight the symptoms; we mistake the symptoms for the disease. We tend to forget the real cause behind the problem, and in our thoughtlessness, we could end up eliminating the very patient, we are supposed to treat!

Therefore, it is essential to find out the cause of the fever, and once it is addressed and duly attended to, the temperature which is after all, only the symptom, will automatically go down. Obviously, temperature is not the disease; it only indicates the wrong functioning of the body.

So we need to see things clearly, before responding; our assessment of the situation must be right. Without a wider and higher consciousness, we cannot have a proper reading and understanding of any situation.

9 Adjustment to Changing Situations

"It is not enough to have a good mind. The main thing is to use it well."

Rene Descartes

If we systematically adopt a fixed adamant attitude, with a pre-conceived and already biased mind, suffering will be inevitable. We need to safely adjust to changing situations.

Although, we do not have to be compromising all the time, a certain amount of flexibility can be helpful. We should not condition ourselves against the flow of life; we would do well in being responsive to new realities.

We must change our attitude with respect to situations. Just like the lenses of our eyes change continuously to better assess and appreciate the vision of any object, we need to adjust spontaneously to unavoidable changing situations.

Our eye-lenses are flexible by nature; they change in shape, especially in thickness – depending on the environment, that is, on the object we focus on. If the object is near the thickness of the lenses increases, and when we are gazing distant objects, such as the stars, the thickness decreases, that is, the focal length of the lenses do not remain a fixed number. Furthermore, the aperture also varies with the intensity of light outside; when there is a lot of light, the diameter of the aperture diminishes, whereas in the absence of light, the aperture becomes bigger in size.

The point is: if the lenses are out of focus, vision will be blurred, and when the vision itself is not accurate, our assessment of the viewed object is bound to be poor. Thus, with a poor definition, whatsoever follows next will be quite obvious – everything will be subsequently wrong.

So, right focusing and adjustment are very important, if one intends to receive anything from existence, and if one intends to keep one's balance. Implacable opposition to adjust to certain situations in life can lead to unnecessary complications.

Sometimes, the original image of an object that we focus on, is itself distorted. For example, reflection on a curved surface – concave or convex – gives a totally distorted image. Of course, we do not take for granted whatever image our eyes see and we do not take things at the face value. In that case, before responding, we need to adjust our minds to get the real picture, not the lenses of our eyes. If the mind itself is not in good shape, the image that we see will be far from realistic; the whole perspective will change. So, to perceive things rightly, we need to adjust both our eyes and our minds.

UNDERSTANDING THE NATURE OF THINGS AND TRUTH 10

The essential seeking since time immemorial has been to know everything about existence — to realize the truth and to unravel the mystery of the universe.

To understand the nature of things and truth requires a certain amount of preparation; one must be open-minded; one must be alert, ready and receptive. Truth is the expression of all the universal laws and principles pertaining to existence. Once the universal laws and principles are known and understood, all the phenomena of nature will no longer remain as mysteries.

Truth does not change with seasons, it is not ephemeral: it is timeless, it is eternal. Facts do not disappear just because they are ignored; the sun does not cease to exist by our closing eyes; the sky is not less blue because the blind man does not see it.

> ***The mysteries of life are revealed to one who keeps his mind vigilant all the time of life.***
>
> *Yajur Veda*

Truth cannot be purchased; it cannot be conquered; it cannot even be taught. Language is too limited to express truth, although words can be very helpful. If we do not come near the truth, most probably there is something wrong with our methods. So, we need to change our methods. In fact, truth has to be caught; it has to be attained; it has to be realized.

Once one is ready to receive truth, it comes on its own. It can be likened to removal of darkness from a dark room when light is allowed inside. One simply has to open the doors and windows to allow outside light to get inside. It would be quite foolish to force darkness out of a room, with closed doors and windows. Sunlight will enter inside automatically, the moment there is no obstacle on the way.

So, to drive away darkness, we must bring in light. But light is visible – only if we open our eyes. A blind man cannot expect to see light by groping only; he will go on groping for ever unless he gets his eyesight.

Even if there are thousands of suns, to the one who is unable to develop eyesight, there will still be darkness around.

The Lost Needle

We look for truth all over the places, except at the right one. We can be compared to an old woman who was doing some weaving work. One night she lost her needle while working. Because the light inside the house was rather dim, she went out of the house in search for the needle near a lamp giving bright light!

Well, anybody can guess the probability of finding the needle outside the house.

So, truth can be likened to the lost needle which we are searching for at the wrong places all the time. It is not to be found on mountains, holy places, on pilgrimages, etc. No, it is within us: it is found inside. To understand the deeper reality of things, one has to go inwards.

With a twisted intellect, one cannot come near the truth. It is like an ant, trying to understand and describe an elephant. One might perhaps come near some partial truth, not the entire truth. But partial truths are also important; when they are understood, they can lead to a much higher truth. So, it is unwise to shut the door, even though the truth is only partial.

> ***"All truths even those which seem to be in conflict, have their validity, but they need a reconciliation in some largest Truth which takes them into itself."***
>
> ***Sri Aurobindo***

Preconceived Concepts and Beliefs

Preconceived concepts and beliefs cannot be gateways to truth. They can neither help to develop eyesight nor insight. Instead, they are hindrances; indeed they act like obstacles on the way to truth; they keep the individual as a prisoner; usually they lead to concomitant sufferings.

Truth comes to one's being when one is thoroughly prepared for it. And to receive it, one has to empty oneself first from inside; one has to decondition oneself; one needs to get rid of all mental barriers and fetters. Then truth will reveal itself, in the unencumbered and unbiased mind. So the inquisitor has to be objective, and objectivity is possible, only if one is aware of one's prejudices. Of course, one has to get rid of one's ego and prejudices, otherwise one will not come near truth; one will be on the wrong track and confused all the time. Thinking with an already conditioned mind cannot be of much use. Unless a dusty mirror is cleaned properly, it cannot reflect effectively. As long as the mind is a prisoner of a system, a belief or a concept, one cannot come near the truth.

Each individual carries in himself a truth that he has to seek and uncover. The seeking has to be done with earnestness; one has to dive deep within. The path he follows to realize this truth, is also the same path that will bring transformation within himself. He does not see it because he has isolated himself from it; he does not really want to know about it, because it may be hard and unpleasant to accept.

So truth is not really hidden; it is not a secret to be discovered; it is as simple as existence. And the secret of existence, if any, is revealed in every leaf, in every flower. The hills and mountains, the valleys and meadows, the babbling brooks and rivers, the woods and the forests – they all hold the secret of existence. However, to uncover anything, to realize anything, one needs to develop both eyesight and insight. One misses everything because one is not genuinely interested; one is too preoccupied with other things.

When a minute speck in the eye can make even mountains become invisible, what to speak of a bigot who is blissfully entrenched in his dogmatic beliefs? He does not see any tree even when he walks through a thick forest. Surely, he is worse than a blind drunkard. Nevertheless, he believes that he is awake and alert! But belief is one thing, reality is another; in his delusion he can never come near the truth. Instead, he will move further away from the truth. The best he will come to, in his blind beliefs is falsehood or a semblance of truth, but not truth in its plenitude.

A person who is blighted by the disease of fanaticism cannot acquire a clear vision; a person who takes a virtual football in a computer screen to be a real football, can only delude himself; a computer simulation is far from the real thing. By the way, most fanatics think that their thinking is objective; but in fact, they cunningly rearrange their prejudices. Therefore, it depends on the genuineness of the person concerned — whether he wants an uncompromising truth or a tinted and counterfeited version of truth.

The problem in this world is that fools and fanatics with a herd mentality are always so certain of themselves; most of the time, they believe they are right; they are convinced beyond doubt, before even experiencing anything. But truth has to be known through personal experience. Believers believe, whereas knowers know. A person of wisdom does not take things for granted; he is aware that there is a deep sea between believing and knowing. Mere speculation about something which, one does not know, is indeed quite preposterous; it can be very dangerous too. How can one blindly believe in something, and also claim to be right? It is not by being sentimental that one comes near the truth. The following quotation is more pertinent now than ever in our strife torn and dislocated world.

> ***"I would never die for my beliefs because I might be wrong."***
>
> ***Bertrand Russell***

Man is a credulous and vulnerable animal; he creates a strong need to adhere to something, to associate with something. Thus, he is prone to brainwashing by unscrupulous predators – the so-called leaders. It is not a crime to follow harmless beliefs, but the problem arises when people are carried away by retrograde concepts of destructive nature; in abysmal ignorance, some are even prepared to kill all those who think differently. So allegiance to such beliefs, inexorably leads to a collective state of atrophied consciousness.

It is not so difficult to give up the practice of unintelligent imitations of others; it is a question of choice. It is only by renouncing the herd mentality that one can expect to grow up.

In the highway of quest for truth, if there is any impediment, the bigot has to blame his or her own deep-rooted bigotry; with coloured glasses and in a prejudiced environment, one cannot come near truth. The highest truth can only be reached by someone with a purified consciousness. By the way, a person who has attained truth is like a perfumer; whoever comes near him gets perfumed too.

Discernment of Truth from Untruth

11

It is for us to discern the truth from the untruth. Sometimes, truth is closely associated with untruth; there is an interwoven complexity; things are neither white nor black; there are more gray areas. Even gray is not of one type; it has various shades.

In some ways, the world may be likened to a river: from a distance, the river looks almost static, but with a closer look, it changes continuously. The river changes every fraction of a second and – it is never the same.

The sun also appears to be unchanging and yet it keeps on changing since existence. Although it has existed for thousands of millions of years, there is an on-going holocaust therein. The heat generated by the nuclear processes is of unimaginable order. Every moment we have a totally new configuration, everything is new and yet it looks very much the same. So perception from a distance is one thing, whereas the reality is completely different.

Similarly, in common parlance, we talk of sunrise and sunset because of what we apparently see. But, in reality, there is neither rising nor setting sun: it is just an appearance an apparent movement due to the relative movement of the earth. The earth which appears to be flat and static, is not so in reality. In fact, for many centuries it was believed according to Ptolemy's theory that the earth was the centre of the universe, and that it was static as well as flat. The sun, the stars and the planets were believed to revolve around the earth. The Vatican church zealously supported the Ptolemaic system which lasted for centuries.

In the sixteenth century, when Copernicus stated that the earth was moving around the sun, contrary to Ptolemy's theory, it was considered as heresy. The church strongly condemned the works of Copernicus. Afterwards, when Galileo confirmed the findings of Copernicus, the former was threatened to death. Galileo was anathemized, as his findings were not in conformity with the church's doctrine.

Naturally, it was not easy to break away from an established system which perpetuated for centuries, to accept a totally different one; it was not easy to come to terms with a new paradigm which changed the very map of the universe. By the way, in India, some 1000 years before Copernicus, it was Aryabhatta who discovered the rotation of earth around the sun.

Now, we know that the earth is a huge globe, in continuous motion, rotating about its axis eastward, i.e. from the west toward the east once in 24 hours; it is also revolving around the sun, once a year. The spinning velocity, that is, the speed of rotation around the equator is about 1000 miles per hour – almost twice the cruising speed of a commercial aircraft! Even that speed is nothing when compared with the revolving speed of the earth around the sun. It is mind-boggling, indeed – about 67,000 miles per hour! And yet, it does not seem to be moving at all. It is just like being inside an aircraft; we do not see anything moving inside because the whole aircraft – with all its contents – is moving.

One thing is certain – it is indubitable: irrespective of wherever we are, we are all passengers in a huge spacecraft by the name of planet earth, in uninterrupted motion, in an ever-changing universe, since the beginning of time.

As a matter of fact, the very essence of the universe is – motion. Every single object, however inert, displays the same nature. Almost everything in the sky is spinning around: planets, moons, stars, galaxies – they are all rotating. So from the biggest celestial body, to the tiniest sub-atomic particle, nothing is really stationary. The laws governing the macrocosm are the same laws that govern the microcosm.

So what appears to be real, is not necessarily so; quite often it is only an illusion of reality. One should acquire the knowledge to separate the reality from the illusion, truth from untruth.

12 Illusory and Insubstantial Appearances

We should not get carried away by illusory and insubstantial appearances. It is futile to run after a rainbow; chasing a rainbow and trying to hold it is unrealistic. A rainbow is not something substantial – one can neither touch nor hold it. It is a natural phenomenon, due to diffraction of sunlight by rain drops. The rain drops act like small glass prisms. A prism has the property to diffract light, that is, to split white light into its components: red, orange, yellow, green, blue, indigo and violet. So with raindrops we get similar spectral effects. And chasing a rainbow is like chasing a shadow.

Similarly, a mirage also is quite insubstantial; it appears to be made up of water, but in reality it is only an optical illusion – there is not a single drop of water to be found.

Mirages are common in very hot weather. A traveller in a desert often comes across what appears to be a sheet of water, just a short distance ahead of him. In fact, there is no water at all – it is only an optical illusion. One does not have to traverse the Sahara desert to experience this natural phenomenon; one can see it on roads on a hot summer day.

The above optical phenomenon is attributed to the refractive bending of light as it passes through successive layers of warmer air towards the ground, that is, from relatively cooler air layers in the atmosphere to warmer layers just above the ground.

In life, mirages of different nature galore; there is no dearth of passing shows and shadows; we are continuously deluded by them because they look glaringly impressive – almost real, albeit misleading. In our wrong perception and approach we go on expecting some sort of happiness from fleeting and illusory phenomena. But the hook remains hidden by the bait.

Very often, we have a tendency to substitute illusion for reality; we take the evanescent for something permanent. But, it is just a fallacy. What is unreal will always remain unreal; the fleeting cannot become ever-lasting. In our delusion, the unreal does not become real; truth cannot be altered. Without proper eyesight and insight, we will be thrown out of balance, for sure.

So, before running after anything one must ascertain the validity of one's action first. Without discerning the illusion from the reality at the very outset, one is bound to be disappointed. By clinging on to insubstantial and transient shadows, we can only expect frustration.

It behoves us to change our approach towards the world; we must not be swayed by worldly phenomena and transitory insubstantial happenings, however seemingly true and delightful.

13

NOT TO JUDGE BY APPEARANCES

Things are not always what they seem. We should not judge too quickly by their appearances. It is erroneous to take things at their face value. It is important to observe and understand things, the way they are, not what they appear to be, otherwise, one is bound to get unnecessarily disappointed.

All that glitters is not gold; a morning dewdrop however sparkling, is not a pearl; all that is black is not charcoal; a book is not judged by its cover; fine feathers do not necessarily make fine birds; beauty is but skin deep; one swallow does not make a summer; all those who claim to be in a position to teach, are not necessarily teachers – many are professional cheaters; the cowl does not make the monk; the wolf in sheep's clothing remains a wolf. Under certain circumstances, even a viper appears like a harmless rope.

A calm lake covered with moss can be very treacherous; the fact that water is hidden by moss and other plants, does not imply that it does not exist. Similarly, the sea does not cease to exist in the absence of waves. If there is no wind, the sea will be silent, and it will be still there – although not very wavering.

Furthermore, on a clear day, the ocean appears blue, when we all know that water is colourless. The blue appearance is the result of the reflection of some of the blue component of light coming from the sky plus the scattering, that is, deflection of more blue rays by the water molecules in the ocean, towards the observer.

Similarly, the changing colours of the sky can be very intriguing to the layman. On a clear sunny day the sky appears to be rather blue, but its colour changes with time and varying circumstances. On a clear day, the sky appears blue because air molecules scatter more blue rays towards us than they scatter the other colours constituting sunlight. So there is no such thing as a blue concrete dome over the earth.

When the sun is near the horizon, as in sunset, we see more of other colours such as yellow, orange, red, etc. The effect is quite visible, when there is a lot of dust particles suspended in the air, because most of the blue component of sunlight gets absorbed before reaching us, and what reaches us mostly is the orange-red component of sunlight. The nearer the sun is to the horizon, the thicker the layer of dusty air which light has to pass through before reaching the observer, the more pronounced is the scattering and the more impressive is the orange or red colour. We see only the orange or red colour because most of the other colours constituting white light do not reach us; they are lost in the scattering process. This scattering effect is known as the Tyndall effect. Indeed, what a fascinating experience to watch sunset!

Now, we know that the sky is neither blue nor red; it is just an appearance due to optical effects. The apparent colour is a function of the density of suspended particles in the atmosphere.

So we should not be impressed by appearances only. We must judge only after full cognizance of the nature of things.

Similarly, we should not be misled by non-appearances – not everything is visible. There are so many things which exist, and yet are invisible to the eyes.

For example, electricity which is due to the movement of electrons in a conductor is not visible to us, but we are very familiar with its applications in our lives. And we do not need to see the actual flow of electrons to believe in electricity.

The same can be said about different types of invisible rays such as: radio-active rays, x-rays, ultra-violet, infra-red, etc. They belie their existence to the naked biological eyes, but their presence can be demonstrated scientifically.

The sun gives visible light as well as non-visible rays. The non-visible rays viz. ultra-violet rays can be very harmful for the eyes and sensitive skin. The eyes should be kept away from direct exposure of sun-rays.

Many gases are invisible, and some of them are extremely toxic. For example, carbon-monoxide and carbon-dioxide – both colourless – are formed by the combustion of carbon-based fuels. Out of these two, carbon-monoxide is very toxic upon inhalation.

So non-appearance also does not imply non-existence; before coming to any conclusion it is important to investigate properly.

Attending to Things in Awareness

14

"It is not by prayer and humility that you cause things to go as you wish, but by acquiring a knowledge of natural laws."

Bertrand Russell

Many a time, we are ourselves responsible for our sufferings, because we do not attend to our duties in awareness. In a state of slumber, we have total disregard for even the fundamental principles. There are certain things which we should not simply contemplate doing, yet we have the most uncanny habit of doing them! And consequently, we end up in undesirable imbroglios; we are caught in webs of our own making. We become wise after the events, but very often we have to pay a heavy and unpalatable price.

If we want to avoid being in such situations, the best protection is knowledge of the natural laws and principles; it is also paramount to attend to things in maximum awareness. Before starting anything, we must have some idea of the finality; before climbing any ladder, it is important to know the number of rungs we have to come across.

We should not put the cart before the horse; we should not start something which we cannot stop; we should not leap before looking; we should not build a wall where a bridge is needed, and vice-versa; we should not throw the baby out of the bath-water; we should not knowingly build castles on moving sands or in the air; we should not count chickens before they are hatched; we should not put all our eggs in one basket; we should not become penny-wise and pound foolish; we should not burn the candle at both ends; we should not throw an arrow that returns with a boomerang; we should not bite more than we can chew; we should not blow and swallow at the same time.

Before clinging to anything we must understand its nature; it is foolish to cling to transitory elements, however enticing. Although the spirit of acquisitiveness is a bit natural, obsessive clinging to money, power, status, etc. is equivalent to clinging to a straw; at the most one can get an apparent sense of safety – that's all.

We must not bank on vulnerable things. Boats made of paper and houses of cards are not better than shadows; they are not different from those found in dreams. After all dreams are dreams. We should not get entangled and carried away just by dreams; we will attain nothing; we will reach nowhere. So attempting to grasp shadows is nothing but a futile exercise, without any shadow of doubt.

Attempting to Do Things with Precaution

Before attempting to do anything, wisdom demands a certain amount of elementary precaution if one is to avoid unpleasant repercussions. One must not scratch the back of trouble.

For example, it would be very foolish to give a dangerous toy to a child and not expect problems ahead. Most children enjoy playing with guns; but responsible parents do not buy real guns for their children, do they? – otherwise anybody can imagine the consequences. Similarly, giving a sword or any dangerous item to a madman is absolute madness; he will most probably hurt himself if not others. The same scenario can be expected by giving a razor to a baboon.

A farmer cannot expect to harvest a good crop if he sows his seeds without weeding out the soil; the plants are not choked by the weeds but by his negligence; he has to prepare the field properly and sow the seeds at the right time. Once all the factors are favourable, sprouting is well-nigh inevitable; he will then have to only wait for the harvest.

We do not start digging a well in search of water, when our house is already on fire; it will be of little use, if any. Water and other means to extinguish fire should be instantly available. By the way, it is only when the well is dry, that we can really appreciate the value of water. Likewise, we do not start reinforcing our house when a 'Katrina' is already on our doorstep.

Whoever sets out to cross an ocean in a sailing boat, must adjust his sails according to the speed and direction of the wind. One who has insufficient knowledge of the sea cannot expect to sail smoothly against the turbulent oceanic currents; the waves and currents are not going to subside because one is ill-prepared. The most probable outcome is a wreck somewhere.

The bottom line is: we do not build statues of snow and then weep to see them melt away.

In spite of all precaution that we take, we do make mistakes in life. After all, it is only human to make mistakes; ignorance and wrong judgements are understandable; accidents happen even in the best regulated families. But we do not respond by crying over spilt milk; we should not be unduly dismayed; it serves no purpose whatsoever. Instead, we must learn from our experiences and from those of others in order to avoid making mistakes in future, but we must try to avoid committing blunders.

> ***To err is human, but wisdom demands that mistakes are not repeated.***
>
> ***Anonymous***

With deeper understanding and awareness, we will attend to things differently.

Nevertheless, most of the time we go on repeating the same mistakes; we do not learn from the past; in delusion, we go on revolving around meaningless things and end up in disillusionment.

It is Important to be Practical and Realistic in Life

15

There are so many things which we should not do and yet, we yield to them, without being practical and realistic. For example, we cannot have our cake and eat it as well; we cannot make an omelette without breaking eggs; much talk does not cook rice; we cannot have both bites of the cherry; we do not kill the goose that lays the golden eggs; we do not see from the wrong end of the telescope for enlarged vision; we do not see the whole sky through a bamboo cane; we do not create music out of a cracked flute; we do not sow seeds on barren granite; we do not keep rotten apples amidst good ones; we do not get tuned in to more than one radio station at a time; we cannot ride two horses at the same time; we do not chase two deers at the same time; we do not search for monkeys on dead trees; we do not catch birds with clubs; we cannot serve both God and Mammon; we cannot make a right out of two wrongs; two blacks do not make a white.

We do not estimate the yield of fruits by the blossoms of a tree. We do not celebrate before cracking the shell of nuts.

The mouth is not sweetened by remembering honey; the sick does not get cured by reading and repeating the name of medicine; the ignorant seeker does not attain truth by just memorizing books by heart.

We must properly knock at the right door; there is a difference between knocking and banging! Truth is not to be found outside; it is found inside, in a peaceful mind. It is only when the mind is still and peaceful that there is the possibility of experiencing the deepest regions. Flowers of peace can only be expected to bloom in restfulness – not in madhouses. However, if the mind is tumultuous, no matter how peaceful the outside environment is, one cannot come near truth.

We should not seek help from something which is itself vulnerable. Someone who is drowning cannot expect to be saved by holding on to a non-swimmer. Similarly, when the blind follows another blind, both will end up in trouble.

One should count life with smiles, not tears. One should evaluate one's garden by its blossoming flowers, not the withering leaves. We do not overlook the fragrance of flowers to give undue attention to the smell emanating from a few decaying leaves.

We cannot appreciate the beauty of a flower by dissecting it; scientific analysis is of no use; it will not reveal anything. We can enjoy its rapturous beauty by contemplating on it; we require eyes for it, not ears. The fragrance of a flower is felt only by coming near it; we cannot expect to get it from a picture.

To see and listen properly, physical eyes and ears are not sufficient. Without the proper technique to develop eyesight and insight, vision and understanding will be very poor.

The ignoramus does not become knowledgeable by drinking ink; the eyesight is not improved by gazing at the sun.

•

The head and heart – both are needed to sail through the countless bends and curves of this material world; one can easily go off the tract with the slightest sign of weakness. The head and heart are to man, what the left wing and the right wing are to a bird.

16

SEARCHING FOR THINGS

When we search for something, we must do it at the right place and in the proper way, if we expect to find what we are looking for. Only if we search carefully, and at the right place that we can expect to find whatever we are looking for.

For example, diamonds are not scattered all over like ordinary pebbles. We must search for them where they are likely to be found; searching for them in a dumping ground is far from a good idea. A lot of digging is required; we have to dig deep within the entrails of the earth.

Only those who dare to dive deep into the sea can expect to find pearls and precious stones. However, we search for firewood on land, not in the expanse of an ocean.

The grass always seems to be greener on the other side of the fence. People have the tendency to search at the wrong places – sometimes very far away – for things that are quite near, in reality. They dream of magical rose gardens over the horizon, ignoring and underestimating the blooming roses in their own gardens. They gaze at the sky for down-to-earth solutions – not further than their feet!

Very often, the behaviour of people is identical to the muskdeer that wanders around in search for the scent produced by its own body.

17

Rendering of Service

Rendering of any service, demands a lot of thoughtfulness and discernment. When rendering any service to the society or anybody, we must ascertain that the service is not misplaced; the party, to whom the service is rendered, is satisfied; there has to be a purpose and meaning behind it. Moreover, the service has to be rendered with grace and promptness. Otherwise, it will become irrelevant; the much intended service turns out to be a disservice. So, if the service is not rendered properly, it will lead to frustration. We should not offer, just for the sake of offering; we should offer what is required.

For example, if we want to help a hungry man, we must give him food, not water. Conversely, a thirsty man can be helped by water, not food.

> *"That action is best, which procures the greatest happiness for the greatest numbers."*
>
> *Francis Hutchison*

We must make sure, that the service offered, is appreciated. Furthermore, whatever charity we give, it should serve some purpose. We do not waste our efforts after imaginary entities; it is of no avail giving medicine to the dead. So, we must make sure that we do not miss our targets.

If people can be taught how to become more responsible and independent, the service will be most meaningful.

"The living need charity more than the dead."

George Arnold

We must also avoid being in a situation of casting pearls before swine; it is then an absolute waste of time, energy, etc. for everybody. The jeweller alone can understand the worth of jewels, anyway.

It is also important to abstain from giving power to hostile forces, if one does not wish to invite trouble. Nevertheless, for the sake of good, one is sometimes compelled to do business with the evil; for the sake of flowers, we have to water even the thorniest plants.

If we want to save a withering tree, we must water the roots, not the shoots.

If one wants to fell a tree, it is not necessary to remove all the branches and leaves. Once the trunk is cut, the whole tree comes down.

One does not kill a tree by cutting off only its branches, as it will not be different from pruning. In fact, such a superficial action will promote the formation of more branches, instead of killing the tree, because its life is not found in its shoots – it is in the roots.

Optimal Conditions for Maximal Development 18

For maximum development of anything, optimal conditions are required. For instance, for a seed to sprout and grow freely under a big tree, it is very difficult. The tree has an over-protective effect. There is too much shadow; there is not enough sunshine. The elements for maximal growth are not in the right proportion. So growth is stunted under such conditions unless the young plant is transplanted in a proper site. For perpetuation of species, seeds are dispersed naturally to a distance from the parent tree.

Similarly, when it comes to upbringing of children, we must make sure that we do not end up poisoning their development by our wrong attitudes. Very often parents tend to be over-protective and too smothering. Overprotection is not necessarily protection from all that is negative; on the contrary, it could stifle growth and life altogether. If we deny them the necessary space for their overall growth, we will be responsible ourselves; and if they get handicapped irreversibly due to our over-caring and suffocating attitude, we can only blame ourselves. In an over-protective society, children can and do very often end up in big troubles. Because they are not simply prepared to face dangers; they fail to recognize the most obvious threats. So it is good to be responsive to their needs, but we must be cautious and responsive too.

Very often, in thoughtlessness, wealthy parents inflict incalculable damages to their own children. For example, by flaunting and displaying their wealth, parents 'succeed' in spoiling their children. The innocent children are brought up in a very artificial world in those affluent societies, and they have the perception that everything is hunky-dory in life. Consequently, in their comfortable home, they end up in becoming delirious and stuporous. Indeed, opulence can prove to be an obstacle rather than a helper.

Perhaps, short-sighted parents will abstain from creating such situations, after contemplating on the following most awakening quotation:

> ***He who sits on the cushion of advantage goes to sleep.***
>
> ***Ralph Waldo Emerson***

It behoves us to provide the right environment for their growth without getting too attached, of course. Over-attention invariably turns out to be counter-productive.

19 For Any Revolution, One Aims at the Roots

For any revolution in life, one has to aim at the roots, not at the shoots.

Man is not a mechanical entity; he is a psychological sentient being. Man's behaviour does not change overnight. He does not change by simple external decorations. He can of course, act and mimic, but to change intrinsically is not so easy – it is a different kettle of fish. For any substantial change to be visible, there has to be a transformation in his inner being – in his interiority, that is, in the roots. To disentangle the clutches of negative tendencies from the psychic and substituting by healthy ideas, however, can be a very slow and gradual process. After transformation, the inner qualities will naturally permeate the body to manifest outside.

> ***"Our life is what our thoughts make it."***
>
> *Marcus Aurelius.*

But without a profound and comprehensive change in the roots, there cannot be any noticeable change on the external surface.

By the way, an impostor cannot betray a good observer. The former can be belied and caught by the aura he radiates.

The aura is just a reflection of what is within us – our feelings and our thoughts. If the feelings and thoughts are calm and harmonious, the aura will be very positive. Conversely, if the feelings are agitated and the thoughts are incoherent, the aura will reflect negative vibrations. Thus, any apparent superficial change will be cosmetic, not genuine.

Incidentally, by simply curbing and controlling the undesirable effects of any cause, we cannot expect to solve any problem effectively. It is tantamount to suppression, not transformation. In suppression or repression, for instance, people can be made to behave in a particular way. But this type of apparent change in behaviour or conduct – with hardly any change in the inner consciousness – is just a pretension. The very ethos guiding the beliefs of a person will remain the same; the negative traits will be still simmering within. At the slightest opportunity, the suppressed person shows his true nature; there is a sudden eruption of his hidden tendencies – the suppressed old habits.

The leopard cannot change its spots, anyway: its distinguishing traits and characteristic features cannot be extricated by superficial means.

The Lion and the Sheep

This is a story of a small lion cub lost in the forest. He was picked up by a shepherd who tried his best to dissociate him from other wild animals. Hence, the cub was brought up in the company of sheep; he was made to change his behaviour and manners. With the passage of time, the lion cub was behaving more or less like a sheep!

Once, another bigger lion which was roaming around happened to notice the strange behavior of the little lion.

He was quite surprised; he tried his best to bring the sheep-like-lion to reason by revealing in the true identity of the latter. He invited the young lion to a nearby pond to facilitate his job. When the little lion saw his reflection and compared with the one of the bigger lion, he was finally convinced that he was also a lion. He also started to roar just like the bigger lion, making all the nearby sheep run away in total confusion. Afterwards, the young lion – convinced of his true identity – decided to follow the bigger lion to the forest.

So, by just some superficial changes and mimicry, a lion does not become a sheep. It is indispensable to change the interiority, that is, the inner pattern, if we really want to see a change in the exteriority. The interiority emerges into the exterior, not the contrary. External manifestations, seemingly positive can be very deceptive. By the way, there are several masks that we wear from sunrise to sunset; by simply changing masks, we do not change: our real character remains always hidden to others.

Very often we manage to deceive others, but the question is: can we go on deceiving ourselves? With a little amount of inward-looking, that is, introspection we will find the answer.

20

No Need to Complain Over Things that are Natural

Very often we have the most unreasonable expectations; instead of accepting things as they are, and reacting accordingly, we think that things in the external world should assume the form and properties, to suit our conveniences. There is no need to complain over things that are quite natural. There is nothing new under the sun.

For example, we wish summer to be cool, and winter to be warm and cozy; we wish fire to be of lukewarm temperature, and ice to be just nicely warm. In short we only wish to be surrounded by niceties all the time. Unfortunately, things do not happen according to our fanciful wishes. If we want to protect ourselves from the blistering rays of a midsummer sun, we must wear appropriate clothes.

Whether we like it or not, we should be familiar with the nature of things, pertaining to this world. For instance, the nature of fire is to produce heat; its very nature is to burn; we must simply learn how to handle it. If we have to extinguish a fire, we do not add fuel to it.

A man who carries a torch against the wind, will most likely burn himself due to his foolishness; he should not be surprised. Similarly if one throws sand against the wind, the result will be quite predictable: particles of sand will land onto the face of the thrower. In a way, spitting against the wind is tantamount to spitting on one's own face.

A dumb fool should not be asked to handle dynamite; he will most probably explode himself /others.

We must handle ice with care as well; we cannot expect ice to be hot. We cannot change the nature of ice; we have to be realistic and reasonable.

We do not waste time in trying to straighten the crooked tail of a dog: it will remain crooked even if put inside a pipe for years.

A horse, which cannot be reined in, a car without brakes, or a life not based on restraint – are all dangerous.

One should not expect a snake or scorpion to display the qualities of a lamb. A snake can change its skin but not its nature. Neither the snake nor the scorpion is to be blamed for our foolishness. They have their own characteristic features; by nature they behave the way they do. The onus lies on us to be on our guard: out of a devil's egg can only hatch a devil.

If we set a wolf in a sheep-fold, and expect everything to be in order, that is tantamount to wishful thinking. Equally, we should not count on a fox to guard the geese. And if we think we can safely rely on a hungry dog to keep watch over sausage rolls, then even pigs might fly.

Where pigs live, it will be dirty; if pigs are brought inside a living room and allowed to stay overnight, it will become a pigsty. Similarly, it is not difficult to imagine the scenario when, an intoxicated elephant is allowed inside a porcelain shop. We should also not be too surprised with the behaviour of unscrupulous wild beasts in the image of humans, who happen to grab power by accident.

So, it is for us to discover the insidious snake in the grass; it is for us to decide with what to associate and from what to dissociate; what to shun and what to welcome; where to build walls and where to build bridges.

We Must Abstain from Denaturing the Nature of Things

21

We must not pervert the nature of sentient beings. We must be responsive to the needs of others. For example, we must not force-feed herbivorous cows with animal derivatives. Conversely, we do not feed inveterate carnivores with Greek salads. A swine used to garbage finds rice less attractive. To a dog even an old piece of bone is more valuable than diamond. So what is food for some, could be poison to others; what is sport to a cat, is a nightmare to the mouse. Therefore, satisfaction is dependent on one's need.

No matter how much attention a wolf is given, it will always return to the forest; a lion can eventually lose its teeth but not its nature.

Among humans also, there is a lot of difference in nature and aptitude. One man's pleasure can become a good nuisance to another. Some people like excitement more than peace; for others peace is more important than excitement. Some highly developed souls are to man, what man is to animal.

Just as delicious food to one man can become harmful to another, the medicine which cures the sickness of one person can become the cause of death to another.

Thus, we must treat people according to their merits; we must learn how to separate the sheep from the goats. We must give the devil his due. And we must ensure that we do not contribute to situations giving rise to square pegs in round holes. Unfortunately, these days, in all walks of life, it is a regular occurrence to come across square pegs in round holes.

We Must not Force the Nature of Things

22

"Look deep into nature, and then you will understand everything better."

Albert Einstein

Too much pressure will burst the tyre. Man should learn to be respectful towards nature. There are certain limits which should not be crossed. Common sense is usually a good guide in this regard.

For example, a person who has the capacity to carry a certain weight, should respect his limitations; he should learn to differentiate between the possible and the impossible. There are certain things which he should simply avoid doing. Any attempt to lift a much heavier weight could be detrimental to his body and health; he could easily damage the discs of his vertebral column; the pain experienced by a person with ruptured discs is far from interesting. By the way, a human being's organ is not a mechanical spare part of an emotionless and lifeless robot; it cannot be removed and replaced without serious repercussions.

We should not expect a donkey to display the qualities of a horse; it is futile to try to change a donkey into a horse by force. One cannot make a race-horse out of a donkey. A donkey is a donkey, and a horse remains a horse.

A lame horse cannot be transformed into a champion by flogging; we should not waste time, energy and effort in trying to achieve the impossible. But, for a good horse, even the touch of a whip is sufficient; he will respond appropriately.

Similarly, we cannot transform a fool into a genius by hammering his brainless head; any effort spent in this manner will be, definitely in vain.

Physical Activity and Sports

It is important to be physically active for the upkeep of health, but one must abstain from overdoing. Any violent and prolonged activity is bound to be counterproductive. Whatever movement one does, one must do it in awareness and gracefully. Sport is alright as long as it promotes a sense of well-being in the individual. However, these days, in the name of so-called sports, humans are trying to imitate animal species in the lower rung of the evolutionary ladder of Charles Darwin, the author of 'The evolution of species.'

Let us consider a cheetah – a four-legged animal. It can run at a speed of about 100 kilometres per hour! There is no point trying to expect the same performance by two-legged animals, because we must compare, like with like. Humans are not four-legged animals; moreover, by virtue of their physical features, humans are totally different sentient beings. Why should they imitate other creatures? Why don't they try to be what they are? They should try to be more reasonable; common sense should prevail.

The grotesque mimicry of monkeys and other four-legged creatures is obviously a far cry from sports. Indeed, such idiotic behaviour is tantamount to descending to a lower rung of the ladder in the biological evolutionary process.

In ignorance and collective madness, people are actively damaging their own bodies – fragile physical structures, after all. Furthermore, some are having recourse to harmful drugs and all sorts of garbage for better performances. In this frantic pursuit of medals, they are prepared to sacrifice even their health. The tragedy is that, instead of rising higher up in the scale of consciousness, humans are hell-bent to go closer and closer, to donkeys and monkeys.

So these days, sports are an aberration; aggressiveness is regarded as something virtuous! The media and even governments are hand-in-glove to promote insanity, on an unprecedented scale. There is an almost irreversible departure from the real spirit of sport, from what we see in international competitions. As a result, evolution – whether biological or in the scale of consciousness – is being suppressed or even negated in the very name of sport. It has to be understood that, evolution is teleological, that is, there is a purpose and meaning behind every design. For continuity of progress, man has to go forward. But we cannot go forward, if we actively try to defeat the very purpose of evolution.

Rest and Sleep

The body should be allowed to rest, as soon as it gives a signal that, it is tired. If the body gets tired, and all the cells within are crying for rest, then we should give rest to the body. It would be suicidal to push physical or mental activities to a crescendo, especially at that point in time.

In order to be efficient, work should be followed by adequate rest to enable the body to recover its energy and strength. Besides rest, sleep is also needed to restore all bodily functions to normal. Sleep recharges the body's battery and helps the various physiological processes of the body – metabolic and catabolic. In fact, a good quality sleep is a rejuvenator too. So sleep is essential for the general well-being – be it physical, mental or even spiritual.

> ***"Extreme business, whether at school or college, kirk or market, is a symptom of deficient vitality."***
>
> **Robert Stevenson**

Antagonizing nature, results in unnecessary sufferings. For instance, a sleepy driver, who is forced to drive, can become extremely dangerous to both himself and others. When one is in a state of stupor, it is better to abstain from performing any activity. Management of sleep is very important; we should pay attention to our bio-rhythms.

These days, night life is becoming very fashionable. Instead of giving rest to the body and mind, people are developing the habit of spending the night in entertainment centres. In those escapades, the body gets exhausted due to lack of sleep and disruption of metabolism, following indulgence in intoxicants and carousing spree. Consequently, there is hangover, atrophied consciousness and loss of strength to perform one's duties during daytime. The loss of one night's sleep results in days of discomfort. So, the problems get accumulated, instead of diminishing.

It seems very few people care to pay attention to the maxim: early to bed and early to rise makes man healthy and wise. Whoever is the one behind the maxim is certainly not a fool; there is a lot of science behind it. As we all know, from the moment the sun starts to set, there is a peaceful atmosphere conducive to rest and sleep – because a kind of peace descends upon the earth. Conversely, when the sun rises, a sort of renewed energy prevails over the earth, and this energy is very suitable for work. Moreover, the early morning breeze brings fresh life to the world. The beauty of the woods, just before sunrise, cannot be described; the spectacle at dawn is unique. The felicity experienced by early risers cannot be expressed in words; it has to be lived to be felt and understood.

One of the most fundamental aspects of living in tune with nature is to respect the diurnal cycles. We do not antagonize the forces that promote our physical and mental well-being. Obviously, all those who go to bed late and get up late, are in blatant contradiction with nature. Their bio-rhythms go berserk and the consequences can be quite damaging for the body. Although loss of sleep may not have a remarkable negative effect in the short term, it is better to establish healthy habits. Anyway, whoever wants to get good drinking water, must do the needful.

Nature cannot be cheated or tricked, without consequences; one has to pay a price for every careless act and for every foolhardiness. So it is better to take heed and have some respect for the forces of nature. Nature is a good teacher; trees, stones, mountains and rivers can teach certain things better than books.

With Changing Parameters, the Value of Things Changes

23

Everything around us has a purpose; we need to understand their value in an ever-changing environment. If misunderstood and misused, what can be helpful, can equally turn out to be a nuisance.

We cannot think of a world without trees; they are ubiquitous. The very nature of trees is to give: trees bring forth flowers and fruits; they produce oxygen – they are the lungs of the world. Any weary traveller in a torrid weather knows how soothing the shade of a tree is. But the same tree becomes a dangerous shelter during a thunderstorm; one does not choose to meditate under it. The fault does not lie on the tree really: in fact, any tree becomes an easy target for the passage of lightning, the more so, if the tree happens to be an isolated one.

Thus, to seek shelter nearby such a tree under these conditions can be very dangerous because the tree itself is threat ened by massive electricity discharges.

A torch is appreciated most in pitch-darkness, not in daylight.

Manure is simply garbage to an office worker but it is gold to a farmer.

A block of concrete on the middle of a road is a dangerous obstacle; it is an accident waiting to happen. However, the same block can be very useful in a different location. For example, it can be used as a stepping-stone to climb a wall.

One Needs not be Perturbed by the Vicissitudes of Life

24

Life is not always a bed of roses; it is not always a spectacle or a feast; not all days are bright and sunny. Man is subjected to the unpredictable behaviour – sometimes very brutal – of things and beings around him. Life then, becomes a test, and the world becomes a place of trial.

But it is quite normal for adversities to come to human beings: they have to be faced simply and squarely as well as with equanimity. Therefore, problems are not things to be deplored; without them life would be too boring perhaps; we must get used to accept both the rough and the smooth. Sometimes, unpleasant events and difficulties can be quite challenging; they are not necessarily a curse; they can be quite salutary because they enable people to grow up. Great achievements usually come through intense pain and grief. Even disease can be a blessing in disguise; it turns out to be a means towards better health!

> ***"Fire is the test of gold; adversity, of strong men."***
>
> ***Seneca***

Many a time, however, we find ourselves caught up by surprise in uninvited maelstroms and we feel like drifting apart, as if we are in a rudderless boat; we lose confidence in ourselves. Instead of reacting positively, we are tempted to give up, without a single fight. We get confused, dejected and become miserable. Instead of strengthening our resolve to overcome the obstacles in our way, we choose to accept defeat. We cannot muster courage to face the situation apparently impossible to tackle. Some people even contemplate the idea of self-destruction, that is, committing suicide!

Despite the nature of the situation, we should not surrender and wallow in self-pity, even in the face of the most trying circumstances. We must not give up the struggle without a good try. Escapism is not a solution; retreat without any valid reason should not be an option. If we can reorganize our energies to tackle the problem with confidence and a positive mind, then it is a different matter. Anyway, if we become strong and wise enough, we can then even convert unfavourable circumstances into favourable ones.

> ***"Mishaps are like knives, that either serve us or cut us, as we grasp them by the blade or the handle."***
>
> ***James Russell Lowell***

Incidentally, in every negative situation there has to be hidden some positiveness waiting for our attention. In every adversity there is an opportunity for the optimistic; a man of wisdom knows how to seize that opportunity; he eventually turns it into a fortune. Emergence of novelty ideas takes place in difficult situations – almost beyond control. The urge for discovery is guided to a large extent by circumstances. Necessity is a great teacher; it is also the mother of invention.

Kites soar to the highest altitude against the wind, not with it. However, for the congenital pessimist, there are difficulties even in an opportunity!

Most of the time problems are relative and subjective; their appreciation depends on peoples' standpoints. So there is no point in overreacting to problems; we must put them in the right perspective. A problem solved properly can keep at bay several others. Indeed, a positive attitude and a good humour can be very helping in dispersing a negative situation. Incidentally, some people have the tendency to create problems out of existing solutions! Consequently, these man-made problems will lead to concomitant sufferings. Be that as it may, a stupid solution to a problem will remain a stupid solution, however apparently successful.

Some people also burden themselves by worrying about trivial matters; they, therefore, waste a lot of time and energy, struggling their utmost to put right, what they perceive to be wrong. So, suffering is not necessarily a fatality – it is optional; very often it is invited.

We must also abstain from exaggerating minor inconveniences into major problems; we must not make a mountain out of a molehill. Small clouds do not herald monsoon floods. Conversely, we must not underestimate the scale of an impending disaster. We must not labour under any delusion and yield to wishful thinking or adopt the ostrich attitude; we must not live in a fool's paradise. By blindly overlooking danger we do not secure ourselves. We must be realistic and react accordingly.

In any event, it serves no purpose to lose our heads; we must keep them above our shoulders. If we yield to tension and panic in critical situations, we will inevitably make mistakes. We must try to remain calm and unruffled; as a solid rock, we must resist getting blown away by the wind; we should not allow storms and tempests to disturb us.

When the going gets tougher, the tough gets going. We must not surrender, however daunting the situation. It is only after having endured the bad that we can experience and appreciate the good.

> ***"He who is fixed to a star does not change his mind."***
>
> ***Leonardo da Vinci***

So we must effectively manage whatever situation, we are in. We are to do our best in whatever circumstances, we happen to be, regardless of any limitation or handicap. With perseverance, a good violinist – even with a snapped string – can still produce music. Unfortunately, it is very rarely that man does the best he can, in any given circumstances. By the way, to do the best also implies to do what is required. If we fall over for instance, it should be for a greater rise, to go further ahead. We must learn from every false step; we must not look where we have fallen but the real cause of our fall.

Problems are not permanent; they come and go. It does not rain all the time, not even in England. We may view trials and tribulations as clouds that screen sunshine from the sun. But the sun is always shining; no cloud, however thick and vast, can stave off sunshine for ever. We all know about the transitory nature of clouds; they have to dissipate sooner or later. It is only a question of time. Every cloud has a silver lining, anyway.

With patience and resolution, we should be able to deal with adversities without losing our balance. Indeed, success becomes satisfying only when one overcomes all hurdles to arrive at the essential, despite unfavourable circumstances. When determined to overcome or achieve something with enough spirit, rhythm and thought, all difficulties are reduced to the level of insignificance. In any case, the roads leading to the heights of greatness are not smooth; they are always fraught with dangers and pitfalls; only after passing through fires, one becomes mature and wise.

> ***"No pain, no palm; no thorns, no throne; no gall, no glory; no cross, no crown.***
>
> ***William Penn***

By the way, we cannot pretend to solve all the problems of the world; the plight of the world will change very little. For example, in situations like bereavements, accidents, financial losses, deep disappointments, etc. we have no choice except to adjust to those difficult phases and come to terms with them; they have been here since time immemorial and they will continue to afflict humanity. It is an absolute waste of time and energy to worry about such inevitable things. Whosoever understands the natural laws, does not cry out against his fate. But there are other situations in which we have the free-will to act, and we should thereby act with all firmness and with appropriate force.

We must also try our best to tackle new problems, and rise above them, should the need arise. We must also prepare ourselves so that we can effectively adjust to changing situations. We cannot reverse the course of events, anyway.

All Times Are Not the Same

In nature, events happen in a cyclic way – changing from one extreme to another. There are high tides and low tides; we have the waxing moon and the waning moon; each wave has its crest and trough. Moreover, every peak has its valley too. After every major catastrophe, there is also a period of relative calm.

In the same way, we have ups as well as downs in life. If good days have passed away, bad ones will also pass away. When things go wrong, it is not the end of the world; all is not gone. The lowest ebb is the turn of the tide. The darkest hour is that before dawn; even the longest night has an ending. Daylight is implicit in every cycle of 24 hours; it has to show itself sooner or later. The emergence of sunrays cannot be suppressed; the rays are unstoppable.

To everything there is a season, and a time to every purpose under the heaven:

> ***A time to be born, and a time to die;***
> ***a time to plant, and a time to pluck up that is planted;***
> ***A time to kill, and a time to heal;***
> ***a time to break down, and a time to build up;***
> ***A time to weep, and a time to laugh;***
> ***a time to mourn, and a time to dance;***
> ***A time to cast away stones, a time to gather stones together;***
> ***a time to embrace, and a time to refrain from embracing;***
> ***A time to get, and a time to lose;***
> ***a time to keep and a time to cast away;***
> ***A time to rend, and a time to sew;***
> ***a time to keep silence, and a time to speak;***
> ***A time to love....................***
> ***...................., and a time of peace***
>
> ***Bible, Ecclesiastes 3: 1 - 8***

So we have to be optimistic. Of course, sitting down with arms crossed and just hoping for things to improve is not the best option; it is tantamount to day-dreaming and wishful thinking. It is said that, the Heavens help those who help themselves; and whoever cannot help himself cannot help others. We must take whatever appropriate steps to get out of any hostile situation, but at the same time we do not worsen matters in haste and thoughtlessness; we do not get out of the frying pan to end up into direct fire nor do we rush into the lion's mouth. Whatever we do, we must act in awareness and understanding the nature of the situation.

By the way, the higher the level of awareness, the simpler our lives become; we become more confident and we advance more towards our freedom. Thereafter, most problems or rather so-called problems, simply disappear.

In A Dilemma one Has to Decide

Very often, we find ourselves in a quandary, and life forces us to make the most vital decisions. Expert advice is not always available; in its absence therefore, we have to decide ourselves. Of course, we do not wish to take regrettable decisions, as far as possible; the difference between being right or wrong at a decisive moment means the difference between success and failure. The decision may not be too palatable, but we have to decide; we cannot go on floundering.

So we go for the best or the least bad, after having carefully weighed the pros and cons. The subconscious mind can be very helpful in illuminating the matter if we have ample time for it. We must learn to hearken to the inner voice. We cannot go on tearing our minds apart, in indecision.

At the end of the day, it is better to take an apparently wrong decision at the right time, than taking a right decision at the wrong time. And once the decision is made, one has to go ahead straightaway without worrying too much of the probably wrong decision made.

For example, very often high school-leavers find themselves in confusion as regards their career in life. Come what may, when one reaches such crossroads, one cannot stop moving. It is better to opt for something rather than awaiting eternity to come to a seemingly right decision.

A bird in hand is far better than a dozen in the bush. One can later on change one's career, if one is not too happy with the first one. At least one will have learned something in life, and with more experience as well as the wisdom of hindsight, one should then avoid making mistakes in future. By the way, judgement becomes better from experience of past errors; foresight gets more developed too. Hence, one can look towards the future with more confidence.

Similarly, a farmer may have preference for a certain type of seeds, though unavailable at the required time. He has to decide, whether to wait for his preferred seeds or not; but if he does not sow his seeds at the right time, he may not have anything to harvest. The same seeds which sprout, when planted in spring, withers away in winter. So, it is better to sow the seeds – not necessarily the choicest at the right time – than to sow the best possible seeds, but at the wrong time.

Be that as it may, anybody who thoroughly understands the nature of things, and is totally aware of his actions – whether physical or mental cannot go wrong. He cannot lose balance; he cannot go off the track.

25

Time and Life

When we think of the universe, both time and space immediately come to our mind. We have been conditioned by a certain linear concept of time; we associate time with the beginning of creation. We think of time as a moving entity – in a continuous motion. It is compared to the flow of water in a river or the passage of clouds in the sky.

But is time a finite entity or is it in abundance? Is it moving somewhere or does it simply exist without any beginning or end?

We are all subjected to time, not vice-versa; time is not subjected to our existence; it is unaffected by our existence or non-existence.

Time may be compared to a vast ocean. Someone who is in the middle of an ocean is free to move about; his movement is, however, restricted because he has a starting life capital, that is, a finite number of breaths. He has the freedom to use those finite number of breaths bestowed upon him in the vast ocean of infinity. So either he spends his breath capital judiciously, or squanders it in worthless movements and activities.

But the ocean is not in scarcity; time itself is not a scarce commodity. Indeed, if there is anything in limited quantity, it is our breaths, our life capital – not time.

Moreover, when we say, "time is money," it would be more appropriate to evaluate our breaths instead. Why? Because time is unlimited, whereas our breaths are not! Indeed, our finite number of breaths may well be regarded as the real sands of time. Logically, time which is in abundance cannot be regarded as precious; it cannot be more precious than our limited number of breaths.

So, time may be compared to an ocean – not a flowing river.

We give a time to our births because it helps to relate with other events. Time is a state of mind within human consciousness; it relates one event to another – past, present and future in a convenient and sequential manner. In our long journey in life, we go through a multitude of experiences, and because of that, we have to conceive past, present and future. And in order to arrange those happenings conveniently, we string them in their sequence of occurrence in our memory.

When somebody is, let us say, 60 years old, we think of the number of years that person has seen up to now. Incidentally, our birthdays are stark reminders of the amount of life already gone. Thereby, it is good to take stock of ourselves and also avoid wasting life on futile things. If a person has not done anything worthwhile in life, we say that he has wasted his time. In fact, he has not paid enough attention to the number of breaths he has squandered; he has mismanaged his life. The question is: has the person wasted time or has he wasted himself?

Indeed, it would be much more appropriate to talk of emaciation by time instead of wasting time, and consumption by time rather than killing time.

> ***"Time conquers all, and we must time obey.***
> ***I waste time and now time waste me."***
>
> **William Shakespeare**

The idea of 'wasting time' is just to convey a certain meaning, in so far as our relation to time is concerned; but the concept should not be misunderstood.

The fact is: we cannot waste time. On the contrary, time wears away everything – even our minds; we cannot stop the process of being wasted by time; nothing can resist erosion by time.

Thus, it is important to know our exact relationship with time. When we think of time, perhaps it would be more appropriate to visualize it in terms of lives and breaths.

So, although time is regarded as money by some people, time is also life. And wasting time is tantamount to wasting life. Indeed, it will be a most foolish thing to waste time or rather one's life for the sake of material gains only. And when in ignorance one gets obsessed by the idea of accumulating wealth, without any intention of using that wealth for the sake of others, then it becomes a tragedy, indeed. Consequently, life is wasted unnecessarily and irreversibly – there is no question of wheeling back.

The Flight of Time!

When we talk of time flying never to return, it an erroneous concept. Time is not flying anywhere; it is not in a hurry to go somewhere. As a matter of fact, we are the ones who are busy going somewhere, without reaching anywhere –

certainly not time. Time is where and as it is; it is not in a hurry at all. So it is for us to change our attitudes; it is for us to see things in the right perspective; we must stop deluding ourselves.

Time and Speed

According to Einstein's theory of relativity, time is related to speed. The quicker one moves in space, the slower one will age. For example, someone travelling in a rocket at the speed of light, will perceive a very slow movement of time. On the other hand, one who travels in a much slower spaceship will perceive a faster movement of time. In other words, each traveller will feel the same given interval of time differently. Thus, the traveller in a fast spaceship will age much less than the one in a slower spaceship - quite intriguing indeed. With this new paradigm, the whole concept of time in space travel has changed.

So, according to the theory of relativity, time is not objective, it is subjective. However, in our daily lives, for practical reasons and by convention, time is an objective reality. The subjective nature will have its relevance, when in some time in future, humans will be in a position to travel in space at the speed of light, that is, 300,000 kms per sec! For the common man, its subjective nature is of very little concern, if any.

The concept of relativity can be grasped in a much down-to-earth manner. For instance, a person undergoing a very unpleasant ordeal will perceive the movement of time, quite differently when compared with one, who is enjoying a very happy event. For the former, one hour will look like one day, whereas for the latter, one day will slip by like one hour.

Times Have Changed!

Times have not changed; if anything has changed, it refers to us, not times. Whether time is objective or subjective, we are not spared. We have changed and are ever changing in the ocean of time. But the ocean simply is, as it has always been, and it will always be. It is the same ocean; it has witnessed innumerable events since existence without itself undergoing any change. The ocean of time has no beginning, no end; it is timeless.

Life is More Precious Than Time

26

The body is important and functional only as long as the soul is residing in it, otherwise it is of no use at all.

Our life span gets decreasing everyday, every minute and every second, and yet all those who are entangled in transitory objects and useless activities are blissfully unaware of it. Man continues to depend upon things that are changing all the time, like the ever-moving shade of a tree. In total unawareness he actively squanders his precious breath capital after futile trifles.

Breaths, however, are means to achieve something much more worthwhile; they are means to propel humans into a higher state of consciousness, in the ascending order of evolution.

What is the use of wasting life for the sake of material gains and comfort only, anyway? True, one has to work to earn one's living. Quite obviously, one has to spend some time while one is working. The problem arises when one ignores the importance of other things, apart from working to accumulate wealth more than required without any justifiable reason.

Life is not a business; it must be seen in the context of time and space. If one can spend money to buy time in life, it would be really most exciting. But, is it possible? The answer is quite obvious.

Thus, one should give up the idea of acquiring money or material gains by hook or crook. Hopefully, the following quotations will shed some more light on the relevance of time.

> *I cannot afford to waste my time making money.*
>
> **Louis Agassiz**

So, the spending of breaths is lot more important than spending money. Money mistakes can be corrected, but squandered breaths cannot be recuperated.

> *The great use of life is to spend it for something that will outlast it.*
>
> **William James**

In life, the main thing is not just how to make a living: the most important thing is to strive to become a superior being; it is to cultivate and develop awareness. So, we must use the remaining breaths – whatever left – in the most judicious manner. Besides, that is the most sensible thing to do. If one has to do something positive, it is better to do it as soon as possible because who knows how soon, it might be too late.

> *Let every dawn of the morning be to you as the beginning of life. And let every setting of the sun be to you as its close. Then let everyone of these short lives leave its sure record of some kindly thing done for others; Some good strength of knowledge gained for yourself.*
>
> **John Ruskin**

PROCRASTINATION–THE THIEF OF LIFE

27

Procrastination prevents us from reaching where we want to. It is said that procrastination is the thief of time. There are certain things which need to be attended at the right time, if we expect to make some progress. We must make hay while the sun shines. We should not put off till tomorrow or the day after tomorrow whatever work we can do today. Besides, waiting for a later time may not give the desired results. For example, one must strike the iron while it is still hot – when it is malleable.

> *"The best preparation for good work tomorrow is to do good work today."*
>
> ***Elbert Hubbard***

Similarly, there are other things pertaining to sentient beings which need to be addressed as early as possible. As goes the saying: one cannot teach new tricks to an old dog. Similarly, an old cat cannot learn to dance.

> *"He that will not when he may,*
> *He shall not when he will."*
>
> ***Robert Mannyng***

People also should be exposed to moral education, that is, human values, civility, righteousness, etc. when they are still young. Manners are best inculcated when the mind is still uncorrupt. Once children get the necessary education at the right time, they will take care of themselves in future. With proper upbringing, one gets the right knowledge; one then displays the right attitude towards others and existence. But once they are grown-up delinquents, with twisted beliefs, it becomes extremely difficult to break away from their deep-seated habits.

> ***"He who neglects to drink the spring of experience is likely to die of thirst in the desert of ignorance."***
>
> ***Ling Po***

Indeed, most of the time, the parents are themselves responsible, inasmuch as they abdicate miserably from their duties as worthy parents. Very often, a wrong step or an omission has an enormous negative bearing on the future of their children. So, it is incumbent upon parents, guardians and all those concerned to attend to their duties at the right time, if they do not wish to regret afterwards. By the way, a small leak could sink a gigantic ship; the repercussions can turn out to be catastrophic; a stitch in time saves nine.

Delaying matters do not pay, but in certain circumstances it is better to opt for a delay than bungling things up. Although it is better to be late than never, unjustifiable procrastination should be simply avoided.

28 Biding Time to Act at the Right Moment

Our journey through life is buffeted by miseries; it may be likened to a boat continually running aground, that is, stuck and wallowing in shallow water. We must bide our time and wait for the right tide to get out of this undesirable situation, as soon as thc opportunity presents itself.

Timely action is very important; it can determine success or failure. After knowing the what and how, it is paramount to know the when. If we do not act decisively at the appropriate time, we will remain where we are. So, it is important to bide time and wait for the right moment.

> ***"There is a tide in the affairs of men,***
> ***Which, taken at the flood, leads on to fortune;***
> ***Omitted all the voyage of their life***
> ***Is bound in shallows and in miseries."***
>
> ***William Shakespeare***

So, the tide must be taken when it comes; one must be prepared for it. Tide and time wait for no man. We cannot ignore opportunities and expect to reach somewhere; opportunities come but do not linger; once they are lost, we cannot reverse the course of events; we cannot wheel back the clock. The water of the river flows on without waiting for anyone.

> *"He who tries to seize an opportunity after it has passed him by is like one who sees it approach but will not go to meet it."*
>
> ***Kahlil Gibran***

So we should not only grasp opportunities, but also create them whenever possible. If not, we will go on vegetating wherever we are. Existence is not the least bothered with our plans; it does not depend on us; on the contrary, we are the ones who depend on it. If we have to go somewhere, we have to act at the right moment.

There is no dearth of opportunities in this world; we can find them, if only we want to. A man with foresight creates more opportunities than he finds, anyway.

29

HAPPINESS–AN ATTITUDE

We all like to be happy. Nobody invites unhappiness. The question is: what is happiness? And where does it come from?

We have the perception that happiness is something extraneous, that is, it comes from outside. Some people think that it depends on one's parents, relatives, friends, career, etc. Any extraneous element might be of great utility in providing a suitable background, but it can neither cause nor prevent happiness. True happiness does not come from outside: it comes from inside us – from within.

When one is unhappy, it is irrespective of the place where one is. Change in Geography or Topography is of no consequence; it is also independent of the circumstances. Moreover, if a certain thing becomes a source of happiness to some people, it may not have the same effect on others. So, that external source whether happiness or unhappiness, is not the real cause. As a matter of fact, it is our attitude that makes us either happy or unhappy. If we think and believe that we are happy, then so we are. Thus, happiness is a state of being; it can be attained only by developing the right attitude.

Let us consider an example whereby, we feel happy in the company of a likeable person. But if for some reason we start disliking the same person, then we become unhappy. Although the person, remains the same, due to our change of attitude we become unhappy. Therefore, happiness comes from within – not outside.

In our wrong approach, we expect happiness from the world; we think the world has to change so that we can be happy. Well, that is a fallacy. It behoves us to change our approach towards the world; we must change our attitudes – within ourselves.

> ***Happiness does not depend on outward things, but on the way we see them.***
>
> ***Leo Tolstoy***

When we are unduly attached to a certain state, we are bound to be disappointed sooner or later, and then experience unhappiness. Since no state remains permanent – nothing remains the same – it is unwise to try to cling to anything.

So when circumstances change, and the changes are not according to our expectations, we become unhappy. As long as we require an external factor(s) to make us happy, we will remain as slaves.

The best thing is to exercise detachment; we must not be swayed by worldly phenomena and transitory objects. We must try to display equal-mindedness – whether in good times or bad times; in honour or in dishonour; in profit or in loss; in good weather or in bad weather, or in any other duality.

> ***Happiness belongs to those who are sufficient unto themselves.***

> ***For all external sources of happiness and pleasure are, by their very nature, highly uncertain, precarious, ephemeral and subject to change.***
>
> **Arthur Schopenhauer**

Now, if an external object truly gave joy then everyone would invariably experience that joy. But we know that this is not so. In fact, an external object giving so-called happiness to some people might be very repulsive to others. For example, some people relish eating aubergines, whereas there are others who simply dislike even the sight of it. Therefore, it is quite clear that happiness cannot be attributed to any external object or event – it depends upon ourselves. The idea of what constitutes happiness and how it can be obtained is misunderstood, unfortunately.

The Search for Happiness

Man is never happy. Happiness is a much coveted state of being; it is considered as probably one of the most important desirable attributes, if not the most important. From the very moment of birth, there is a yearning for happiness. Most of our actions are in some way or another geared towards its pursuit. Some people strive hard to become happy, yet most of the time they do not get the expected results. It is a fallacy to find happiness when the approach itself is wrong.

> ***The foolish man seeks happiness in the distance, the wise grows it under his feet.***
>
> **Robert Oppenheimer**

One should not hunt happiness directly; the pursuit of happiness, as an aim, is ridiculous; it should not be the objective. Happiness comes as a by-product; it comes as a consequence; it comes as a reward if we deserve it. Once the actions are right, the consequences also have to be right; the fruits of harvest have to be sweet. For example, one invariably experiences happiness by rendering service to others. But we cannot just look for the reward without deserving it, that is, without walking the walk! It is only by mistaking the consequence for the aim of life that people end up in miseries, instead of happiness.

Whosoever by his unrighteous behaviour is causing suffering to others, cannot expect to live in peace and happiness; one cannot be truly happy at the expense of others. The treasure trove of happiness remains hidden by negative thoughts and deeds. For example, if somebody has committed a heinous crime, it will be difficult for him or her to lead a happy life, because the criminal action will keep on hounding the person's conscience, all the time. One may commit a crime, but may not be free from its consequences in the inner world. So it is absolutely necessary to abstain from indulging in wrong actions. Happiness cannot be experienced by a mind with a heavy conscience.

> ***Happiness comes when your works and words are of benefit to yourself and others.***
>
> ***Siddharta Gautama***

In our modern society, we find ourselves struggling all the time to gain economic security. We tend to believe that money and material possessions can make us happy. However, people who spend all their lives accumulating wealth, in the end, get totally disillusioned; they realize their mistakes when it is already too late. The tragedy is that, even after realizing their mistakes, very few people have the audacity to take remedial actions.

True, some people do manage to buy some comfort as well as some pleasure – but not happiness. Happiness cannot be bought in any supermarket: it is not found in finite material things or in their multiplication. All the money in the world cannot buy happiness.

Although comfort and pleasure might be an apparent source of happiness, they are non-lasting – they are illusionary too. Happiness cannot be attained by self-gratification; it cannot be equated with comfort and pleasure. While pleasure and comfort are dependent on the five senses, happiness is not.

The more the comfort, the less is the happiness. Indeed, by relinquishing cumbersome possessions, any sensible person would feel much more at ease. To be without some of the superfluous possessions, one is much lighter and happier. Admittedly, a certain amount of basic comfort is important for the well-being of man, but it is quite childish to think that one will be freer from troubles when one is surrounded by luxuries. Opulence is not the key to freedom and happiness.

In any case, comfort and pleasure are quite relative and subjective. One person's pleasure can be a good irritant to another. For example, some people find pleasure in strange activities such as killing innocent animals and even human beings! Most incredible, and yet it is a very sad reality.

Some people try to get happiness by consuming harmful drugs! This is indeed, a real tragedy. While drugs may induce some sort of euphoria, certain desirable feelings, by acting on the central nervous system, they have nothing whatsoever to do with happiness. It is common knowledge that, addictive drugs, can only wreak havoc in the body; not an iota of happiness can be obtained by using such substances. Yielding to such things is tantamount to giving more power to negative forces.

Pleasure can be derived through different means. For example, we can derive it through relationships, through achievements, by eating and drinking, etc. Be that as it may, pleasure is always dependent on some factors. It can be illustrated by the following: Let us consider an exothermic process, that is, one that produces heat. The process could be a chemical or a physical one. Whatever it is, in an exothermic reaction, heat is not produced on its own. All the ingredients have to be there; the conditions have to be right. Heat production will continue, unless there is interference.

The experience of pleasure is a bit like an exothermic process. Nevertheless, there is a difference: the very source of pleasure can also become irritating – when there is too much of it. The same process which gives rise to pleasure becomes unpleasant and even repulsive when prolonged for a long time; the same vibration becomes undesirable. So pleasure will eventually lead to pain, and that sort of pleasure should not be mistaken for happiness. Anyway, if we make pleasure the aim, then pain is a condition attached to it; the two are inseparable. Be that as it may, the conquest of desire for any elusive pleasure brings more happiness than yielding to it.

Happiness is not something far away; it is neither in the horizon nor in the zenith. The real source of happiness is the mind; it comes from within and it is based on peace and a clear conscience; it is an inner flowering of what is the best. Only a calm, relaxed and detached mind can experience happiness, hidden inside; it is a straight runway for bliss. Thus, happiness is attainable, provided we do the needful. It is a bit like the sun, hidden by clouds on a cloudy day. The clouds consist of negative thoughts, endless desires and unwarranted anxieties. Unless we disperse those clouds, we cannot experience happiness. When the mind is agitated, there can be sorrow only. So, the treasure trove of happiness is always there – whether we are aware of it or not. It all depends on what we really want. The distance between heaven and hell is not greater than a single thought.

> ***"The mind in its own place and in itself can make a heaven of hell, a hell of heaven."***
>
> ***John Milton***

Happiness and Material Things

We live in a material world and everything around us is transitory in nature –undergoing change in one time scale or another. We are supposed to use matter to our benefit without becoming one with it.

Material wealth is a blessing if it is managed judiciously. It is not a sin to be rich as long as there has been no double-dealing or cheating in the process. Wealth obtained through rightful means should then be used intelligently.

In the pursuit of wealth, man has lost his own self; instead of assuming the role of a master, he is behaving like a slave. He is so caught up with the frenetic idea of accumulating wealth that, nothing can check his ever-growing appetite. He simply wants to be ultra-rich overnight – whether by hook or by crook. He does not realize that by trying to possess all types of worldly things in the pursuit of happiness, he inexorably gets more and more enmeshed, entangled and imprisoned into a lot of trouble. Instead of freeing himself, he keeps on creating more chains around himself. Finally, he finds himself locked in a prison of his own making.

What is the reason for such madness? People tend to equate material wealth with happiness. If that were true, all the rich people would have been the happiest in the world. But in reality, they are far from being the happiest.

In fact, they have a tendency to cling to their wealth irrationally; they constantly live in insecurity – with the fear of losing what they possess. Indeed, the sense of ownership can be a big problem; it reduces people to slaves and watchmen. So, the price one has to pay to carry around the weight of an inordinate wealth is far from pleasant. The keepers of wealth are more often possessed than its possessors.

Some people, however, spend their whole life accumulating material things: no amount of accumulation can make them content; even the abundance of the world will not suffice for them. Greed keeps them forever poor and unhappy. In fact, the more they have, the greater is their desire to have more. Is that the meaning of happiness? Certainly not. It is indeed very strange the attitude of the wealthiest people, when the more so, they are fully aware of the cause of their unhappiness, that is, over-attachment to their possessions. Well, peace and happiness cannot be felt when one is not at ease; peace is not achieved by just hoarding more wealth.

In any case, wealth or money is a dynamic force, that is, it cannot be possessed by somebody for eternity. Those who have it, are only its guardian – not possessors. Unfortunately, only a few people realize the deceptive-mirage nature of wealth. Therefore, there is no point in getting over-attached to it. If wealth is available, it has to be used judiciously. Neither a greedy accumulation nor a reckless squandering is good.

We must adopt a reasonable attitude towards wealth. We must understand that all wealth belongs to existence. Indiscriminate piling up of things more than our needs is not going to make us happier. Unfortunately, most people cling to wealth foolishly and selfishly without any concern for others. Wealth beyond one's capacity to handle is harmful; it can take away one's peace of mind, and it can also increase one's ego. Of course, that does not mean that people can be comfortable if they live in abject poverty – surviving under miserable conditions. It is very important to strive to improve one's living conditions.

> *He who knows that enough is enough will always have enough.*
>
> **Lao Tze.**

Worldly treasures cannot make a person great: only character can make someone great. Wealth can decorate a house, but only virtue can decorate a person; dress can decorate the body, but only conduct can decorate the person. Moreover, there is a great beauty in simplicity.

Anyway, a good name is like a fragrant ointment; it is far better than riches. Material gains are after all, only transitory, and instead of wasting time after them, we should aim at something more worthwhile. We should move from the grosser material things to the subtler world; we should aspire towards freedom and perfection of the whole being.

According to Aristotle, the great Greek philosopher, happiness has nothing to do with money; it is a question of how one behaves. We do not need to lead monastic lives and chant mantras all the time to find true happiness; asceticism is not a necessary condition of life. We must try to know ourselves and find our balance.

In his acquisitive frenzy, man is running after the shadows; the substance he is missing lamentably. Instead of becoming happier, he ends up in lot more anguish and misery. The solution is: simplicity and content. He should pay attention only to things that will help maintain himself.

Anyway, the purpose in life is not to grab whatever pleasure one can get, but to evolve to the highest level of consciousness; it is to move forward from imperfection to perfection. Therein we will get, true freedom and happiness.

The runway of happiness is found within, not in the thoroughfares of the gross material world.

30 Too Much Goodness Becomes Harmful

Anything, however good, becomes undesirable after a certain limit. Food is essential for life; it repairs and builds up new tissues. However, one ends up with all sorts of health problems when one overeats. So, the same life-supporting food, when abused, becomes a poison.

Some people have the habit of gobbling up whatever they can, from sunrise to late night, without realizing the harm they do to themselves. It is a common feature in the modern society, especially. Modern man is eating too much, too richly and too quickly. But the quality of life does not improve by overeating; moreover, longevity is not proportional to gluttony. It is said that, only one third of what great eaters consume, keeps them alive, and the other two thirds, keeps the doctors alive!

There are so many other things we add to food to enhance its taste and flavour. Examples are: salt, sugar, spices, etc. Among all additives, salt and sugar are the most common ones. They are not strictly 'foods' yet they are regarded as indispensable commodities and a must in every kitchen. We cannot imagine cookery without salt. Nevertheless, salt eating is an addiction; it is disastrous for health; it creates havoc in the body. It opens the door for high-blood pressure, kidney problems, liver disorders, edema and other degenerative conditions.

Similarly, sugar is another addictive chemical. We all like sweet eatables and drinks, but processed and refined sugar as well as sweets and candies must be avoided. Over-consumption of sweetness can bring a lot of bitterness in our lives – obesity, diabetes, heart diseases, blindness, etc. And these days we have plenty of sweet junk so-called foods in the market.

We must therefore, be very careful with our intake of salt and sugar. Both of them are dangerous chemicals. Indeed, they are silent killers; they wreak havoc in the body insidiously.

So whatever we consume, we must be mindful of the consequences. We might be impelled by the desire to overeat tasty foods, but by trying to consume beyond measure, we will ourselves get eventually consumed in the process. Thus, a cause of pleasure can also be a cause of suffering: to avoid health problems, it is better to eat wisely.

The same principle applies in other matters. For example, even the best music becomes an irritant if heard too often. Similarly, wealth enables us to buy our needs, but an obsessive accumulation of wealth without any purpose invariably leads to suffering. Wealth can be very useful provided it is managed judiciously – with a sense of detachment. In the end, too much of it becomes a burden; it has to be discarded, anyway.

So the key to everything is: awareness. Whatever we try to do, it must be in awareness and with full cognizance of the nature of things. Without a thorough knowledge of truth, whatever thought we contemplate on and whatever action we undertake to accomplish will be inevitably flawed.

❑❑❑